PENGUIN BOOKS

THE EFFECTIVE WAY TO STOP DRINKING

Beauchamp Colclough is a qualified and internationally respected therapist who has helped countless people from all sorts of backgrounds end their dependence on alcohol. He worked for several years at a treatment centre in Kent and now works with his wife in private practice in London, where he treats various forms of addiction and emotional problems.

He has worked with alcohol addiction all his life. Born an alcoholic, he decided to change his life through abstinence from alcohol.

D0587983

BEAUCHAMP COLCLOUGH

THE EFFECTIVE WAY TO STOP DRINKING

PENGUIN BOOKS

PENGUIN BOOKS

Published by the Penguin Group
Penguin Books Ltd, 80 Strand, London WC2R 0RL, England
Penguin Putnam Inc., 375 Hudson Street, New York, New York 10014, USA
Penguin Books Australia Ltd, 250 Camberwell Road, Camberwell, Victoria 3124, Australia
Penguin Books Canada Ltd, 10 Alcorn Avenue, Toronto, Ontario, Canada M4V 3B2
Penguin Books India (P) Ltd, 11 Community Centre, Panchsheel Park, New Delhi – 110 017, India
Penguin Books (NZ) Ltd, Cnr Rosedale and Airborne Roads, Albany, Auckland, New Zealand
Penguin Books (South Africa) (Pty) Ltd, 24 Sturdee Avenue, Rosebank 2196, South Africa

Penguin Books Ltd, Registered Offices: 80 Strand, London WC2R 0RL, England

www.penguin.com

First published by Viking under the title *Tomorrow I'll be Different*, 1993
Published in Penguin Books 1994

7

Printed in England by Clays Ltd, St Ives plc

To Peter and Annabel, for showing me another way to live.

To Josephine, who saw a future and helped me find it.

To Davey, who never got this far.

Contents

Contents

My thanks

To Arlene Kelman, for training me (like only she could).

To my secretary, Jill, who has taught me discipline in getting a job done, and for typing the manuscript of this.

To all the therapists I have worked with throughout the world and the self-help groups that have so openly shared their ideas and hopes with me.

The questionnaire on pages 23–5 has been adapted from Robert Lefever's *How to Identify Addictive Behaviour* (PROMIS Books Ltd). The poem on page 47 is from *Knots* by R. D. Laing, copyright © The R. D. Laing Trust, 1970. Reprinted by permission of Tavistock Publications.

Preface
by Elton John

I have been sober, clean and abstinent for two years and one month now. Without doubt these have been the best two years of my life. I no longer drink alcohol, take drugs, eat white flour or sugar, and I no longer purge myself bulimically. If this sounds pretty drastic – and it is – well, it had to be. By 28 July 1990 I was in a terrible mess. Riddled with addictions, I was obese, miserable, suicidal and beaten. Until then I thought that I could cure myself of all my troubles. I *knew* I had major problems, and I could not stay clean or sober for any length of time. Everything I did was 'on my own terms'. That is, I frowned on people who went to therapy, had treatments or consulted psychologists. It was, in my opinion, a sign of total weakness. 'Can't they get themselves together without all that?' I used to think.

The level of denial and false pride within me was enormous. As I refused all offers of help I slid further and further into the abyss. Hell on earth. So what happened?

I fell in love with someone who wanted to get help for their own addictions. They went to treatment and I visited them. I freaked out there, and got very angry. I fled back to England and locked myself away for two weeks. However, I knew that this person was trying to tell me something, and I knew what it was: if I didn't act quickly I was going to die. It was that simple. I went to visit my friend again, and we had a brutal confrontation. This time I was ready to listen, and I decided to seek help for myself.

When I made the decision to fight for my life, I began to change emotionally and spiritually. First I decided it was time to confront my own behaviour, and I went to a hospital in Chicago. There I was treated for alcoholism, cocaine addiction, compulsive overeating and bulimia. During my six-week stay I learned how to get honest, to communicate with other people and, most importantly, to forgive myself. 'No one beats up on Elton like Elton' was a slogan that had to be put to grass.

I truly believe that communication is the greatest form of therapy – to tell someone how you feel. I was *numb* before I went into hospital, but I began to talk – and write – about my life, and now I am in the 'thawing-out' process called recovery. Today I am grateful for my life – I am no longer wasting it. I realize how precious life is, and how lucky I am to have been given another chance.

Beechy has been a soul-mate since I left Chicago – he has seen me on a regular basis and we have become dear friends. He always emphasizes the positive side of my character: he has encouraged me *to be me* and not be apologetic about it. I am now convinced that those of us too proud, too arrogant or too frightened to ask for help need people like Beechy to nourish us and help us claw our way back into existence. I would personally like to thank him for his love, kindness, compassion and honesty. It has helped me so much. If your life is out of control as mine was, I know that this book will help you.

August 1992

Introduction

My first introduction to alcohol was sitting upstairs in the house where I lived as a child, looking out of the front-bedroom window towards the top of the street, to watch for my father coming home, at about 10.30 to 11.00 p.m. Sure enough, at about that time he'd appear. More often than not my mother would be there with me, because she'd want to see the way he was walking. Would he be unsteady on his feet? Would he be straight as a die? Or would he be with some of his drinking cronies and being loud and noisy, carrying further supplies for the remainder of the night?

These three different conditions were very important to my mother and me, because they would determine what sort of night we were going to have. If he was unsteady on his feet, it would mean that he'd pick arguments with my mother, bang doors and shout. If he was walking straight, it would mean that we had in store a complete history of the family and how they'd survived over the years. My mother and I would have to sit and listen attentively, but however hard we listened it would never be good enough: there would always be faults.

If he was with some of his cronies, this would mean that my

1

mother would have to cook. 'I'm hungry,' he'd say. He and his friends would sit and drink and talk and talk and talk. I'd go to bed, or I'd be allowed to stay up for a while and listen to them talking about nothing, with no one really listening to anyone else. One minute they'd argue, the next they'd be laughing, and this would go on for most of the night until they left or passed out.

The following day my father would be up early again, shaved. I always knew when he was going to have a drink: he didn't smoke cigarettes when he wasn't drinking, so when I smelled the tobacco in the morning I knew that he'd be off again. For him it was never a question of going out for a couple of drinks: he'd go out first thing in the morning and come back last thing at night. Many a time my mother would try to deter him, first asking him not to go, and later going to the pub to persuade him to come home. He, of course, would promise her that he would. 'I'll be there in twenty minutes,' or 'I'll be there in half an hour,' he'd say, but he never was, so we'd sit upstairs and watch for his return.

Looking back, I realize how little attention and affection I received from my father and how his moods were engineered by his drinking and not drinking. For years I blamed him for what I became, but I have since come to realize that he suffered from something that made him behave like that – something called alcoholism, or alcohol, or drinking too much, or whatever name you want to give it. I know that it 'took' my father, and the end result was never pleasant. Alcoholism was like a thief in our lives: first with my father, who after all was a creative and talented man (though I don't think I ever saw the real him), and then later on with me.

When I sat and watched my father, I quietly made a vow to myself that I'd never be like him. I'd never drink (I remember how I hated the smell of alcohol on his breath) – not me. I wasn't going to be like him or behave like him: when I married and had children, I'd be a good husband and parent; I'd be responsible and not break promises. How ironic it was that my first marriage was destroyed by my alcoholism and by my subsequent irresponsible and selfish behaviour. I couldn't help what I became, but I regret how time and time again alcohol came first and everything and everyone else took second place.

While I vowed, 'I'll be different,' I was so full of ambition and hope for the future. I remember having a set of drumsticks and practising with them on the back of a plate for hours and hours on end. I also remember the thrill of my first drum kit – one of the few things my father bought me. I treasured it: I so wanted to be a drummer in a band.

So, when people say to me, 'How much experience do you have with alcohol?', I tell them, 'About forty-four years' – I was born into it, I was brought up with it, and I have been on the receiving end of the behaviour brought about by it. Also, I have suffered the consequences of my own behaviour. I understand people with drinking problems because I'm one of them.

I can remember wondering *why* my father used to drink alcohol, because he never seemed to be happy or to be enjoying himself when he was drinking. He may well have been while he was in the pub and with his friends, but I certainly never saw him a happy man. I also remember watching him the day after he'd been drinking and seeing his hands tremble and how physically ill he would look. What confused me even more was that he *never* drank every day: he was a 'binge' drinker, and would often go months without a drink, although even then he seemed as if he was just waiting to drink, because he'd always seem very depressed and bad-tempered. I'd then find myself wishing that he would go for a drink, because I never knew which was worse – him sitting at home moping without one, or him at home under the influence. The effect on me was confusing: I never knew where I was with him or how to behave – I could never please him. I never brought friends home – I wasn't allowed to. I couldn't understand why he behaved the way he did, and I felt hurt by his criticisms of me – I used to think, 'Why is he doing this? What have we done that he behaves like this?' For a long time I used to think that it was my fault. For years I blamed him and resented him, but not any more. I've come to forgive him, because I have come to know that he suffered from an illness and he had no choice in his behaviour once he started to drink.

Though I used to look at him time and time again and say, 'I'll never end up like you; I'll never behave like that,' I was wrong. No matter how much I promised I'd not be like my father, alcohol seemed to be just waiting for me, just waiting for me to pick it up. From the very first time I did, I loved the way it made me feel. I loved the effect, even though the first time I did have a drink I was sick – probably because the stuff that I was drinking was like congealed tarmac. (It didn't have a label on the bottle. How could it? – there was nothing good to say about it.) Nevertheless, I liked the way alcohol made me feel. It seemed to take away the insecurity that I suffered from – it made it easier for me to talk to people, and in some ways it felt such a comfort. It was as if I'd been standing out in the cold for a long time, and someone had come and given me a coat. I put it on, and it felt warm and comfortable, and I felt content.

At the start of my drinking, that was what it was like. Alcohol was a very good friend. It wasn't a problem. In fact I enjoyed drinking, and I wasn't the only one doing it – it seemed that everybody I knew was drinking, and that that was the thing to do. That's how it started. I'd found something that helped me to have more of a personality. It helped me to communicate with people better (I thought), and, as I said, it seemed that everybody I knew was drinking – especially at weekends. We'd go out to a bar, go listen to music, get 'a couple of bottles', and go back to someone's home and sit drinking and talking and enjoying ourselves. But it didn't take long before alcohol started to mean a lot more to me.

I joined a band as a drummer. To start with we played locally, and then we moved further afield. Really it was then that my drinking started to affect me in a different way. I had come to depend on it more and more to help me cope with playing before large audiences of people – that was something I found difficult, but alcohol seemed to remove my fear and my nervousness, and bit by bit it started to creep more and more into my day. It wasn't so much something that I needed to use to play better, it seemed that I was using it more to function better. All of this I realize today, but back then as far as I was concerned drinking was just something that I enjoyed doing. Certainly alcohol made me feel good, and I wanted to feel good all the time. The band I was with continued to play, and we did very well and became popular. That meant that I was earning more money. Consequently I was able to drink more, and by this time I had started to use drugs too.

I started to use a lot of amphetamine – 'speed', 'sulphate'. I also dabbled a lot with LSD. But, more than anything, alcohol was my favourite, because it was legal – all the other drugs were illegal. Around that time, smoking cannabis, hashish and pot was very popular, but I could never really get into that. I couldn't see the point of smoking something and then just falling asleep (which was the effect it had on me), so I really never bothered much with smoking dope. As I said, hashish was illegal, alcohol wasn't, so I decided to stick with the legal drug. As time went on I did use drugs, but not to the extent of my alcohol abuse.

I continued playing with the band, and as far as I was concerned I was having a really good time – we were playing at lots of different places, and I couldn't think of anything else that I wanted to do. My drinking stepped up a gear when the band went on a tour of Europe. We were working very long hours in clubs and American army bases, and most of the day and well into the night was focused on alcohol. There was always a party to go to or someone who wanted company or someone to talk to, and there was always a drink to go with it.

By this time I'd started drinking in the mornings. I can remember to this day sitting in a little hotel room I was sharing with a guy called Davey (a member of the band): if we didn't have any alcohol left from the night before, one of us would go to the shops close by to get some. It really didn't seem all that abnormal to be doing that at 8.00 a.m., or sometimes even earlier if I was awake. We used to make jokes about having a 'liquid breakfast', and a 'liquid lunch', and a 'liquid dinner'. Life seemed so full of music and good times . . .

. . . and some bad times – like when our agent didn't pay us at the end of the month, and we'd find ourselves sleeping in an empty van or on the floor of a garage or an army base. Even if we (or I) hadn't got the money, we'd always get a drink. There'd always be a soldier or someone who would buy us a drink. Food was secondary by now: alcohol came first.

At the end of that tour the group split up and I joined another band. They very quickly noticed how much I drank, and there were continual arguments about it, until one day we had a meeting and they informed me that they'd found someone else, because they couldn't continue with me playing and behaving the way I was. I got very angry with them, because I didn't want to hear what they were saying. I told them where to stick their band and everything that went with it. When people asked me what had happened, I blamed it all on the band – I said that they were boring, miserable and straight, and I didn't want to stay with them. Nothing could have been further from the truth.

Around that time I met up with my friend Davey again. He started talking to me about the Channel Islands – somewhere I'd really never thought about. He said that he was going to go over there to get some work – picking tomatoes, or some other kind of seasonal work. He said that it sounded like good fun, and wondered if I would like to go along. At first I didn't fancy it: I thought, 'Why would I want to go picking tomatoes?' It wasn't until Davey said that the alcohol was cheap and the pubs were open all day that I really started to think seriously about it. It didn't take long for me to make my mind up. I promptly sold my set of drums, and we set off the following day.

That was the start of many wasted years – years that consisted of drinking, losing jobs, losing friends. I can't say 'losing relationships', because I didn't even know how to have one. I travelled around Europe with a bag on my back, wandering aimlessly from place to place with no direction in my life. I'd end up in hospitals to dry out from my alcohol abuse, and I'd come out of the hospitals feeling healthy and fit. But what would be the first thing that I'd do then? I'd have another drink. In a very short space of time I'd be right back where I started. People got tired of telling me what I was doing to myself, because I'd always shrug it off and take no notice of them.

The first person I took notice of was an American friend of mine named Gary. (Around that time I'd also met someone I'd started to care for a lot, and I knew that if I didn't do something about my drinking I'd lose her.) Gary told me that he knew two people who'd be able to help me if I was prepared to listen to them.

That afternoon he took me to their house, and he introduced me to Peter and Annabel. I didn't realize it then, but those two people were to save my life. I remember sitting in their home with both of them talking to me, and everything they said was so true. They warned me that continuing to drink the way I was would kill me – I needed to do something about it once and for all. I remember making some comment that I'd cut down my drinking, but they told me that I needed to quit: my 'cutting-down' days were over, and the only way I was ever going to save myself was to stop. I left their home feeling very frightened and angry: frightened because what they'd said had touched a part of me, and I knew they were right; angry because they'd told me I had to stop drinking, and it seemed that this was taking something away from me. How crazy.

I phoned my girlfriend and told her that I'd been to see them, and that they'd suggested taking me to a meeting of a self-help group. She was more excited than I was. (I can understand that, because she was very worried about me. It was the same old story – everybody worried about me, and me not worried about myself.) I went to the meeting of the self-help group, and there I heard other people talking about their problems with alcohol. They might have been talking about me: everything they said I could understand; everything they had done I had done too. But there was also something very different about them, and that was the way they were talking: it was so honest and without bullshit. That was something I was not used to.

I left there feeling very positive and excited, but it wasn't long before a little voice in my head became very strong and said, 'Well, you can just have a couple of drinks and go to the meetings, and bit by bit you can cut it down.' So that's what I did. I continued going to the meetings and I continued drinking – but it wasn't a couple of drinks. I felt hypocritical and dishonest. I'd go to the meetings and tell the people there that I hadn't been drinking, but they could tell very easily by the look of me and by the smell of my breath that I had. However, the one thing they didn't do was reject me: they just let me ramble on.

One Thursday evening I was at one of these meetings, and to this day I don't know what happened to me there, but I'm grateful that it did. I admitted openly that I'd been drinking, that I'd never stopped drinking, and that I couldn't take any more of it. That was the first time in my life that I'd ever asked for help. Annabel asked if I was prepared to go for treatment, and I said that I'd do anything.

The following Sunday morning I found myself sitting on an aeroplane with Peter and Annabel, being taken to Plymouth in Devon, to a treatment centre – Broadreach House. I didn't know what I was getting into, but I quickly found out. The information came from a woman named Arlene Kelman, who told me that she was going to be my counsellor. I didn't know what this meant, and the whole thing felt very strange, and I was very frightened. But I also felt very safe, because the warmth from the people at Broadreach was very different to anything I'd experienced before.

After about my fourth day of being there, I started to withdraw from the alcohol. I went into the 'DTs' – something I'll never forget. It was so frightening. I was continually hallucinating, and I lost all idea of time and where I was, but I can still remember that voice in my head saying, 'Get out of here. Have another drink. Get away from this place.' But, even if I'd wanted to, I couldn't – I couldn't even get out of bed. The care that I received got me through that, especially from one of the nurses, named Carole, who stuck it out with me when it got really bad. I had about five or six days of that, and then, as quickly as it had started, it had gone.

That was when the treatment started. For the first time in my life I had to take a look at what I'd been doing, and that's where Arlene came into all this. She guided me, supported me, cajoled me and rekindled the sense of humour that I thought had died in me a long time ago. She kept telling me that if I quit drinking I'd make something of myself and my life would change beyond my wildest dreams. I used to look at her and think, 'Is she really serious? Does she really believe this?' She did, and she was right.

Six weeks later I was back in Guernsey, stone-cold sober, feeling like a little lost boy, but also feeling something else – something that I'd never felt before – and that was as if I'd started something. For the first time in my life I'd been honest: I'd talked about myself, faced up to myself, and actually admitted that I was an alcoholic.

That was the beginning of my recovery. I knew that I was going to have to fight hard to get back my self-respect and the respect of other people. That didn't come overnight, because there were so many who'd heard me say so many times before, 'This is it – I'm going to do something with myself,' but every time I'd said that I'd ended up drinking again. So I had to start from scratch.

The first thing I had to do was to find a job. Around the time I'd got back from treatment, there was a new hotel opening in Guernsey – The St Pierre Park. It had been advertising for kitchen assistants (a fancy name for dishwashers). I rang up and got an interview, and I went along to see the personnel officer. Having had washing-up jobs before, I found it very strange to go through an interview, so this made me quite nervous. Also, I was sober, and I wasn't used to doing anything without a drink. However, the personnel officer (Dorothy) was extremely nice. She asked me some questions about what I'd been doing for employment. Straight away I ran into difficulties, because one of my biggest fears was having to tell someone what had actually happened. When she said to me, 'You're thirty-five years old. How come you want a job washing dishes? What have you done with your life?' it was the first time I'd had to tell anyone that I was trying to pick up the pieces of a life ruined by alcohol, and that I was trying to make a new start. Well, luck was on my side, because she gave me the job. It felt so good to have actually done something for myself, and even better that I had done it without a drink.

I'd been working there for about six or seven months when I learned that there was a competition – the *Salon Culinaire* – taking place, and most of the chefs in the hotel were entering different dishes to be judged by a team of chefs. Well, standing in the corner of the kitchen of the brasserie where I worked (merrily washing dishes), I fantasized about what it would be like to enter the competition. All of a sudden a voice came into my head saying, 'Why don't you ask the head chef if you can enter?' I thought, 'No, I can't do that,' but the voice said, 'Oh yes you can! Go on – do it!' So I did. I left the brasserie and went upstairs to the main kitchen, where I found the head chef in his office, looking very severe and writing out menus. I knocked on the door and went in. I said, 'Excuse me, Chef, but I'd like to ask you a favour.' He grunted at me. He was a large Austrian who didn't seem to smile too much, but he was a wonderful chef. I proceeded to ask him if I could enter the competition, and he looked at me rather quizzically and said, 'But you're a kitchen porter! You have no experience.' I tried to tell him that in the past I'd worked in different kitchens, and sometimes I'd been able to help in the

13

preparation of the food, but he didn't want to hear that. He told me to go back downstairs and to get on with my work. I felt so bad on the way back to the kitchen – I was angry, hurt and ashamed. All the old feelings came back. I felt so silly for asking. 'I should have known better,' I thought.

Later on that evening, at about 9.30 p.m., the phone in the kitchen rang. It was the head chef. (I think he'd had a few glasses of wine.) He said, 'Yes, you can enter the competition – there's one dish left. Come up after you've finished.' I was so shocked, and the first thing I thought was, 'Serves you right for asking.' I instantly became very worried. At 11.00 p.m., after I'd finished washing up and cleaning the floor of the kitchen, I went upstairs. There they all were in their lovely white chef's uniforms and tall hats, and there was I in my kitchen porter's pinny. I reported to the head chef, who told me that he wanted me to make six different hors-d'œuvres, and that one of the larder chefs would give me some ideas. The rest of the chefs found it very funny that a kitchen porter should be allowed to do this, so there was a lot of mickey-taking, and they found it rather amusing that I was actually serious about attempting this.

Attempt it I did. It took me about four hours, and it's just as well that people weren't sitting in the restaurant waiting to eat these hors-d'œuvres or they would've died from starvation. At about 3.30 a.m. I'd finally finished, and my hors-d'œuvres were put in the fridge to be taken down at 8.00 a.m. to the hotel where the judging would take place.

The following day was my day off, but of course I went to the hotel to have a look at all of the entries (and also to have a look at mine). When I walked through the front door of the hotel, the first person I saw was the head chef, though I didn't recognize him straight away because he wasn't in his chef's clothing. He took me by the arm and led me into the ballroom where all the food entries were, and he led me to mine. I got the shock of my life, because there beside it was a small card reading 'Second Prize'. I was speechless. I was totally overwhelmed. I couldn't believe that I'd won a prize. For the first time in my life I'd finished something. I felt so proud of myself that I nearly cried – in fact I think I did cry.

From that day on, things really started to change for me. I was moved from washing dishes and cleaning the floors to the preparation of food in the brasserie. One day a week the hotel also sent me on a catering course. One afternoon I was asked to go to the catering manager's office. When I got there, the head chef was with the manager. They said that they wanted to put me in charge of the brasserie. Again I was speechless and totally overwhelmed. I couldn't believe that this was happening to me.

So, from washing the dishes and cleaning the floors, I went to being in charge of a kitchen and to wearing the chef's whites with a tall hat. It was like a dream come true. I was actually being given responsibility, and people were trusting me.

Another day-dream I'd had, which had started while I was in treatment, was to be a counsellor and to be able to help people with their addiction problems. I'd been working at the hotel for about two years when I had a phone call from Arlene Kelman – my counsellor at Broadreach House. She asked me if I would like to train with her to be a counsellor. Once again I couldn't believe it: all the things I'd wished for were actually happening to me. I went to Broadreach House and trained for two years, and then I met Dr Robert Lefever – the founding director of The PROMIS Recovery Centre, where I now work.

From the moment I met Dr Lefever, I loved his energy and his willingness to be spontaneous and to try new ideas. For the past six years we've worked closely together, and it is he who has given me the support to put my ideas into practice. He has also given me the opportunity to train on both sides of the Atlantic.

I hope that through this book I can pass on to you some knowledge and information to help you too to gain the happiness and freedom from the abuse of alcohol that you deserve. I am living proof that tomorrow you too can be different. Here's how to do it.

PS If at first things don't work out for you, don't be too hard on yourself – it takes time to conquer alcohol, but if you want to you will.

Be aware

If you have been drinking consistently,

you must seek the advice of your doctor

before ceasing drinking completely.

1 What, me?

Quite frankly, the fact that you're looking at this book means you must be concerned in some way about your drinking, even if a lot of you will be reading this book in the hope that you'll learn that you don't have a problem.

I'd like you to make a promise to yourself: that you'll read this book right through to the end. If it helps, keep this to yourself for the time being, as you may feel less pressure. I hope that eventually you'll reach a stage where you make a decision that's really positive for you.

Please don't dwell too much on the word 'stop', which is on the front of this book, or on the phrase 'give up drinking'. You won't believe me now, but I want you to know that 'stop' really means the start of something better than you'd believe possible at present. I think my own story shows that. Giving up is really about saying goodbye to something that's got in your way and that more than likely has caused you many problems and much pain in your life.

So who is likely to have a drinking problem? What do problem drinkers look like?

- Will they have a job, or family, or friends who care?
- Do they have ambitions, education, talents, self-worth?
- Will they have been booked for drunken driving?
- Do they ever gain promotion at work?
- Can they be doctors, nurses, schoolteachers, airline pilots, company directors, vets, bus conductors/drivers, psychiatrists, surgeons, priests, nuns, ministers, social workers, athletes, footballers, students, models, shop assistants, mothers, fathers, sons, daughters, aunts, uncles, taxi drivers, musicians, journalists, editors, writers, students?
- Can they come from any walk of life?
- Do they have to have nothing in life?
- Is it possible to have a drinking problem and to be loved by friends and family?

In fact, a person with a drinking problem can be anyone – not necessarily a tramp on a park bench, or someone from a poor, uneducated background: such people constitute only a small number of problem drinkers. A person with a drink problem will often be someone who society, in general, would not suspect of having any problems. If you have a drinking problem yourself, you know that the real amount which is drunk by a problem drinker will not be spoken about. Some drinking may even be done secretly – and I'm not necessarily talking about using hip-flasks or keeping alcohol in the car: it may be an extra drink taken when someone is out of the room, because for some reason you don't want people to know how much or how frequently you're drinking. Please also realize that an alcoholic has to start somewhere. The amounts drunk may not be huge, but the feeling of being driven is something that you can't explain, and sometimes this may perplex you.

Don't be fooled into thinking that a problem with alcohol means that you necessarily drink in the mornings and every day. That's an old myth – probably created by those of us who have been scared to admit our problems, and who say things like, 'Well, at least I don't drink in the morning,' or 'At least I'm not drunk every day.' Be aware of that incomprehensible feeling of having to have a drink. You may fight it – for days, weeks or months sometimes – to prove that you can control your drinking, but also consider that intense relief when your first drink is consumed after that period of abstinence.

If you feel that you have to count drinks, or not to drink for a while because you've repeatedly drunk too much, don't you think that sounds like a problem? What about those who repeatedly drink and drive when over the limit? Why is it so hard not to drink when you know you have to drive? Have you ever found yourself drinking when you really know that you shouldn't? You may be looking after small children for a friend, or have an important business meeting to attend where you know you'll have to be on your toes; or you may need to use your car – and something takes over. All reason goes out of the window, and you have to have a drink – or drinks.

If you have a problem, you'll also be wondering what the nature of this problem is. You'll ask yourself, 'How come I can achieve most things in my life – I'm intelligent and able – and yet I have virtually no long-lasting control when it comes to alcohol?' The answer is that a problem with alcohol cannot be sorted out by reasoning. It's an addiction. Beating yourself up by calling yourself 'weak-willed' and 'pathetic' will get you nowhere. You need to understand the real nature of this problem in order to find a way out (if that's the path you wish to take).

I should think that by now you're getting the message that there's no clear-cut answer to what or who is a problem drinker. Let me help you start to look at *you*, and where you are with alcohol. I could focus on the number of drinks you take, but I think that could be misleading. Also, the strength of your favourite drink should not confuse you – people who just drink lagers and beers can still be problem drinkers: just because you don't drink spirits doesn't mean you can't have a problem. And don't fool yourself that if you only drink champagne and the best wines then you can't have a problem. And don't blame situations for your drinking.

All I ask is that you think carefully about each answer to the questionnaire below, and remember at this stage that you don't need to discuss your answers with anyone. If, however, you have any health concerns, I'd suggest that you consult your doctor immediately.

Before you look at the questionnaire, think back over the time you've been drinking. You may have been concerned about the way drinking and alcohol are affecting your life for a long time. Please remember one thing: problem drinkers can be totally respectable people. Don't focus on those you may know who you think are worse than you. So what if they are? It's you who's important, so stop kidding yourself.

Let me give you another important tip: this problem hides in the very denial of itself. What I mean is that you may well be suffering from something that tells you that you haven't got it. Recently I spoke to someone who was kidding himself that he was only drinking two glasses of sherry. What he didn't say at the outset was that the glasses he drank from were virtually four measures. So if you know you have to kid yourself, take stock.

Before you answer the questionnaire, make a decision that for the first time in your life you're going to be honest with yourself about your drinking.

---

1 Do you find that having one drink tends not to satisfy you, but to make you want more?   Yes/No

2 Do you tend to gulp down the first drink fairly fast?   Yes/No

3 Do you almost prefer to drink alone rather than in company?   Yes/No

4 Have you often had a drink last thing at night to help you get to sleep, or had a drink when you wake up in the middle of the night?   Yes/No

---

5 At a time when you'd anticipated having a drink, would you have one even though the only drink available was a variety that you don't normally like? Yes/No

6 Do you like to drink a little and often throughout the day? Yes/No

7 Do you tend to use alcohol as both a comforter and a strength? Yes/No

8 When you have definitely drunk too much, do you tend to feel defiant as well as disappointed in yourself? Yes/No

9 Do you tend to time your drinking so that others are not really aware of how much you're drinking? Yes/No

10 Would you have a drink before you go out to a function that might be teetotal? Yes/No

11 Would you find it strange to leave a half a glassful of your drink? Yes/No

12 Do you find that feeling lightheaded is often irrelevant in deciding when to stop drinking? Yes/No

13 Do you have an absolute rule not to drink before a certain time of day, or have you ever given up alcohol for a week or a month or more in order to prove to yourself that you could do without it? Yes/No

14 Are you aware from your own experience that you
commonly drink significantly more than you intend?   Yes/No

15 Are you consciously determined and generally proud
of your ability to control your drinking?   Yes/No

16 Have you committed two or more drink-driving
offences?   Yes/No

17 Have you lost two or more jobs or positions of any
kind because of your drinking?   Yes/No

18 Has anyone else ever expressed repeated serious
concern about your drinking?   Yes/No

19 Have you ever had a complete blank of fifteen
minutes or more in your memory when you tried to
recall what you were doing when you were drinking
on the previous day or night?   Yes/No

20 Are you worried about your drinking?   Yes/No

See page 242 for the key to this questionnaire.

2 Alcoholics don't come in bottles: they come in people

Can you imagine going into a pub and spending £8 or £9 each evening for four or five nights in the week? You go into a pub, spend the money on the alcohol, and nothing happens. You don't feel any different. You don't get merry, and you don't get as drunk as you used to. You feel exactly the same as you did when you walked in.

At closing-time the landlord calls 'last orders' and you have a couple of large ones, and still nothing changes. Would you, in all honesty, continue to do that? Would you go into the pub so often and spend so much money?

If you are having trouble deciding (which I doubt), I am worried for you. Of course you wouldn't spend £8 or £9 a night, four or five nights a week, if nothing was happening to you, if you weren't *feeling* any different at the end. That, after all, is why people drink: why I used to drink and why you drink. It helps you *feel* different.

I don't know about you, but drinking certainly made me feel more confident. It made me say a lot more, and it gave me the impression that I was very funny: I could tell a better joke than the next person and could chat up a girl better than most of my friends. It gave me a lot of Dutch courage. I felt sociable. Of course, I used to get so sociable I couldn't speak and I'd fall over. I'd throw up all over the place.

But that's me. How about you? How does alcohol make you feel? Do you experience some of the feelings I am talking about?

- Does drink make you feel more confident and sure of yourself?
- Does it help you to confront situations differently?
- Does it relax you?

Is it a reward for working so hard through the day – for doing the garden – for doing the shopping – for looking after the kids?

What I am saying to you is this: alcohol changes the way you feel.

Alcohol acts as many things. It can act as a friend, a comfort, a strength. The funny thing is that you've got strengths already: you can do the things that you think alcohol helps you to do, but you just need to get yourself into a different frame of mind, and get a different sort of 'energy' around you rather than having to drink to help you experience the feelings you want. Although alcohol is quite popular in any case, if it alone really produced all those feelings, it would be even more popular.

So we agree: alcohol changes the way we feel. For some people, that's fine. They can go to a pub, have a drink, and walk away. Can you? Can you walk away, after one drink? I used to say I could, but I couldn't. The only place I would walk to after one drink was the loo. Then I'd walk back to the bar again. Or maybe I'd have a drink and move to another pub ... then another ... then another. But I could never have just one drink.

That's me again, but how about you? If you can have just one drink, that's wonderful! Well done – enjoy it! If you can't – if you've got to have two or three – then maybe we have to look at what it is that you want and feel, and why you can't feel like that *without* having a drink.

Human beings are feeling animals. We like to change the way we feel.

- We like to feel positive (at least most of us do).
- We like to look nice, and we like to be told that we do.
- We like to play sport and win – we like to come first.
- We like to be clever.
- We like to be liked.
- We like to be seen as being good people.
- We like to feel good.

If something such as alcohol changes the way we feel, of course we will drink it. Like any relationship, the relationship with alcohol is always wonderful in the beginning because there is a warmth and a bond.

Have you ever noticed in pubs how many people stand on their own, saying nothing and apparently lost in their thoughts? The only movement they make is to have a drink. Nine times out of ten it'll not be a soft drink – it'll be alcohol, which helps them relax. It helps them to day-dream and fantasize.

It's wonderful to fantasize. No one says 'No' in a fantasy. After a few drinks your mind can wander to being tomorrow's hero – a wizard – to imagine being successful without having to make any effort.

At the beginning of this chapter I asked if you would go back to the pub each evening and spend all that money if nothing changed. Isn't it funny that you never see soft-drinks bars where people gaze into space over an orange juice, a bitter lemon or a Coke? There's a simple reason for this: soft drinks don't do what alcohol does.

Have a look at the diagram on page 30 – it shows you what happens. You start off in a 'normal' state, you have a couple of drinks, and something changes: your mood swings. Alcohol starts to widen your thoughts – at least in the beginning. You drink your quota, you start experiencing things, and then you come back to your normal state when the alcohol has left your body. So of course there doesn't seem to be any threat at the start. Drinking is a very sociable thing to do. You like the way it makes you feel – and why shouldn't you? You know you've enjoyed a nice experience; you're not breaking any laws; you can drink in pleasant surroundings –

The effective way to stop drinking

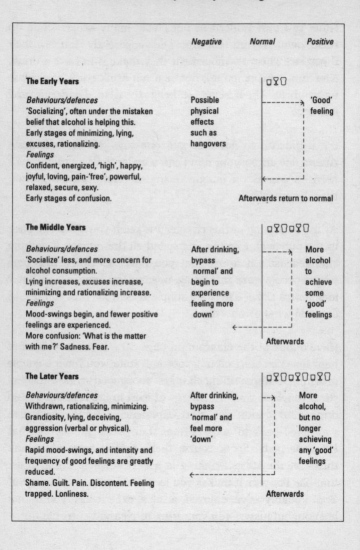

	Negative	Normal	Positive

The Early Years

Behaviours/defences
'Socializing', often under the mistaken
belief that alcohol is helping this.
Early stages of minimizing, lying,
excuses, rationalizing.
Feelings
Confident, energized, 'high', happy,
joyful, loving, pain-'free', powerful,
relaxed, secure, sexy.
Early stages of confusion.

Possible
physical
effects
such as
hangovers

'Good'
feeling

Afterwards return to normal

The Middle Years

Behaviours/defences
'Socialize' less, and more concern for
alcohol consumption.
Lying increases, excuses increase,
minimizing and rationalizing increase.
Feelings
Mood-swings begin, and fewer positive
feelings are experienced.
More confusion: 'What is the matter
with me?' Sadness. Fear.

After drinking,
bypass
'normal' and
begin to
experience
feeling more
'down'

More
alcohol
to
achieve
some
'good'
feelings

Afterwards

The Later Years

Behaviours/defences
Withdrawn, rationalizing, minimizing.
Grandiosity, lying, deceiving,
aggression (verbal or physical).
Feelings
Rapid mood-swings, and intensity and
frequency of good feelings are greatly
reduced.
Shame. Guilt. Pain. Discontent. Feeling
trapped. Lonliness.

After drinking,
bypass
'normal' and
feel more
'down'

More
alcohol,
but no
longer
achieving
any 'good'
feelings

Afterwards

either in a pub or in your own home – so what's wrong with feeling some joy and happiness and a little bit of confidence? If you feel warm and loving, there's nothing wrong with that. You're not doing anyone any harm. You're not doing any harm at all, *if you can stay like this* – if you can *enjoy* your drinking.

But if it's different for you – like it was for me – something starts to go wrong, and it doesn't take for ever to happen.

If you look at the middle of the diagram, you'll see that, having found this new source of energy and comfort, you've drunk more alcohol. Again you've experienced pleasant feelings, perhaps of achievement and pride, and you're sometimes quite overwhelmed with the surge of feelings. You'll have experienced some side-effects too, but they won't have been unpleasant enough to stop you drinking . . .

Until, maybe, the first time you got drunk. This also seems to be all right in many circumstances, but for you it may have been different. You may have found that, just before you got drunk, you behaved in different ways: ways in which you really wouldn't have behaved had you only had a couple of drinks. Think about this. Think back to the way you behaved.

Put down the book for a couple of minutes and think about the first time you really had too much to drink and went over the top. You may not be able to remember all of it, because you probably experienced a 'blackout'. I'll talk about that later on, but just think about the situation you were in.

On reflection, was being drunk that great? Was it that wonderful to behave like that? Were you physically sick? What was the hangover like (if there was one), and what did you feel like? Did you say, 'I'll never do that again'? Did you feel any remorse? Did you want to listen to your friends telling you things you couldn't remember: 'God, what happened to you last night?', 'Did you drive home?', 'Do you remember what you said to those people? Why did you behave like that? You suddenly changed . . .'

Can you remember those things being said to you? Isn't it strange that you experienced this with your 'friend' – alcohol – and yet you continued to drink? Isn't that odd? I always liken it to having a bucket of petrol, someone setting it alight, and you sticking your hand in it: you scream because it hurts so much. What do you think people would do if you continually did that? What would they think? They would think you were crazy.

But you carry on. Somehow you seem to get deluded that it won't happen again, that you can control it. Well, maybe you can control it – for a while.

Then it seems to take another twist. You have some drinks and then you leave that stage of normality (or however you were feeling before you drank). You get excited again, and get into a state of intoxication. When the alcohol wears off, you come back. But you've changed a little bit. Things don't seem so normal. You don't feel so good, and you haven't brought that nice experience back with you. You seem to be feeling something else: maybe the negative feelings in the middle of the diagram come into play a little bit more. Have a look at them.

Do you experience some of these feelings? If you do, it means that alcohol isn't doing the job any more. Maybe it isn't taking you where you want to go.

Has anyone ever commented, 'Why were you late the other morning?', 'Why were you late for that meeting?', 'Why didn't you turn up for the football match?', 'How come you behaved so strangely?' Have you used any excuses? Have you not told the truth? Maybe you've externalized the problem, or rationalized it. Can you remember that? Try to jog your memory. Did you say:

'Oh well, it was because of something else, and I really tried but I had to do this, that or the other'?

Or did you minimize it:

'Well, it wasn't all that important'?

Or did you just deny it:

'I can't remember saying I would do that. I can't remember making that arrangement'?

You see, something has started to change, because you wouldn't normally do that. You wouldn't normally tell lies, even if they are, as you see them, 'little white lies'. It's like anything else: when a relationship is good, people will comment, 'You look happy. You look *really* contented. Something must be working for you.' So why wouldn't they comment when they see you not looking and feeling so good, or acting strangely? If they care for you, of course they'll comment. Of course they'll say something.

Let's go back to the diagram again. You just seem to carry on, don't you? You make excuses and people accept them – for now – and you continue having what you call 'a few drinks'. I think by now it's become more than a few drinks, because you have to have more to feel the way you want to feel. Even though you have a few more drinks, you don't feel how you want to. You're not experiencing the high, overwhelming, fulfilled feelings. Instead, there seems to be a sense of sadness, fear and despair coming in.

You may not want to acknowledge it, but really that's what's happening. Of course, in the meantime you're stuck in the middle of the diagram defending yourself.

One of the things that bothers me is that I used to believe the excuses. It frightens me that I actually started to live a fantasy, when reality was still going on all around. As you can see from the diagram, you're buttressed by these defences, and somewhat alienated from reality. This again will get in the way of you seeing what is happening to you.

It seems pretty normal to want the initial good feelings. Why would you ever want all the other stuff, though? But then I'm not talking about a normal situation: I'm talking about something that alcohol seems to be producing for you. Remember what I said earlier: everything starts off OK, and it's nice, and you have many good feelings. But the game has now changed somewhat. You're now having feelings of despair, guilt, shame, sadness, remorse, fear, anger; the feelings of being trapped, alienated or lonely. Why is it, then, that you continually try to get rid of these feelings by drinking, even though it never works? Don't you think it would be common sense to just stop doing it?

But you're still living in the hope that you'll get back those feelings you used to have when you first started drinking. However, because of the progression that I've outlined to you in the diagram, that can never be the case. You can't go back. So, if you've been identifying with some of the feelings I've talked about, you'll now be getting the picture of what's been happening to you when you use alcohol.

Let me give you an assignment:

Get a blank piece of paper nd draw out the way alcohol first made you feel (like I have the diagram). Put down your feelings and what has been happening to you. Also, draw a circle with you in the middle, and put in your own defences, or how you have been coping with what people have been saying to you. Please be as honest as you can. You don't have to show this to anyone else unless you choose to, but if at this point you

are considering making some changes around your drinking
habits you may want to involve someone you trust. I'll leave that
to you.

It's now very important for you to understand that you are a
feeling person, and that you had all your positive feelings
long before you started using alcohol. So, you don't have to
rely on drink. Drink only gives you a false feeling of confidence, of self-worth, of belonging, of being a good person, of
being worthwhile. There is another way.

First, though, we have to identify what's happening. So carry
on with your assignment and see how your experiences
compare with the pattern in the diagram. We'll go back over
them later on in the book.

3 It's not the amount you're drinking, it's the wanting to drink

Ask most people for their definition of an alcoholic or someone with a drinking problem, and nine out of ten of them will say that it is someone who drinks vast quantities of alcohol. They'll also say that alcoholics drink every day, morning, noon and night, that you're likely to find them begging in the street, sleeping in stations or shop doorways, that they're all unemployed or unemployable, and that they don't want to do anything about their problem. That's the view of most people when they are asked this question.

I'm saying that you *do not* have to drink vast quantities of alcohol or to drink all day to have a problem with it. Nor do you have to drink every day, to be begging in the street or to be sleeping in stations or shop doorways. You don't even have to be unemployed or unemployable.

There's a strong belief within society that you have to drink a lot to have a problem, but I'm saying that it's not the amount you're drinking, it's the wanting to drink that's the problem. I'm talking about the preoccupation with alcohol: thinking about when your next drink is going to be, thinking about lunchtime or when you'll have finished work so you can get the alcohol on the way home (by calling into either a pub or an off-licence), looking forward to having your first drink at home with dinner or, after you've eaten, settling down to watch television with a bottle beside you. Whether or not you finish the bottle is not the issue: it's the whole pattern that develops that's important.

Every problem has a pattern that goes along with it, and a drink problem is no exception. It may be that you don't have your first drink until 7.00 p.m., but ask yourself: are you doing it every day? What would it be like not to do it? Try it! See how you feel. Many people with drinking problems delude themselves by thinking that, because they drink in certain ways, they don't have a problem. You could very easily say to me, 'There's nothing wrong with me, Beechy. I only drink beer.' Is there a difference between beer drinkers and spirit drinkers? Yes, there's a big difference: beer drinkers take in more fluid than whisky drinkers, so they'll probably spend more time in the toilet. The plain fact is that alcohol is alcohol, and it doesn't matter how you mix it: drink enough of it and you'll become drunk.

Some people say they never drink before 5.00 p.m., or only after 10.30 p.m., or never on a Saturday or Sunday, or only on a Sunday. It's obviously better if you do have some control over your drinking problem – you're definitely better off than somebody whose drinking is completely out of control – but the point is this: normal drinkers have nothing to control. They don't care about where or when they drink, because it's not a problem. Ask a normal social drinker, 'When was the last time you had a drink?' and they'll probably not remember

– not without thinking about it – because drinking is not an all-important issue to them, so they don't think about their drinking history. They don't spend time thinking about when their next drink is going to be. When they want a drink, they'll have one – without making up all the excuses and lies that you have to. Of course, the more excuses and lies you tell, the more difficult it is to stop doing it. Once you fall into a pattern of behaviour, it's hard to break it.

You would think that, having reached this stage, it would be easy to recognize that there is a problem, but most people with a drinking problem don't see the problem like other people see it. Consequently, when they're confronted about their behaviour, they'll deny it. More often than not they'll minimize it by saying, 'I'm not drinking all that much,' or 'I'm not drinking every day,' or 'I'm not drinking until the evening.' But can you see what's happening? Can you see the pattern? If you're not drinking that much, what's the problem?

Why do you have to lie and continually deny something if you're not doing it? The reality is that you're denying doing it because you want to keep on doing it, because you're probably dependent on it. The emotional comfort you get from alcohol is driving you to continue this behaviour, not just the social aspect of it. What started off as social drinking now seems to have turned into habitual drinking, though it doesn't have to be heavy. As I said earlier: it's not the amount you're drinking, it's the wanting to drink that's the problem. It's the craving for it. It's the taking comfort in knowing that alcohol's there even without having started to drink it.

Have you noticed your reaction when someone says to you, 'Don't have another drink,' or 'You can't have another drink,' or 'I've thrown the drink down the sink,' or 'I've given the drink away'? Think about what your reaction is like then. It probably turns from anger to rage. Why would a comment like that be a problem if your drinking is not a problem? Dependence is about *needing* something, about *wanting* something. It's about not being in control of your emotions unless you use something to change the way you feel. Once this dependence is formed, it's not easy to break. It's not easy to get off this cycle, but it is possible, and the first step in doing so is understanding what's happening. Hopefully, by reading this book you're beginning to get a picture of why you're behaving in the way you are.

I can't teach you how to drink like 'a lady' or 'a gentleman', or however it is that you wish to drink. I can't show you how to do that because you are one of those people who cannot drink like everyone else. Think back to the last time you had too much to drink. Can you remember how bad you felt, physically, emotionally and mentally? Can you remember the way you behaved or said, 'I'll never do this again – I'm definitely going to quit or cut down'? And then the next time you had a drink it happened all over again.

I think by now you should be realizing that your behaviour is not suddenly going to revert to how it was when you first started drinking. It is going to change, but not in a very positive direction. What started off as social drinking progresses to occasional relief drinking. From there you go on to constant relief drinking. There'll be an increase in your alcohol tolerance, so you'll drink larger quantities, and in your estimation you'll not be getting so drunk. There'll be an urgency for that first drink, and a craving for the next drink. There'll be a total preoccupation with where that next drink is going to come from and how you're going to get it without going through the now familiar hassle of making excuses to people.

If you're a car owner, you'll more than likely be driving under the influence. You'll have feelings of guilt about your drinking, your memory blackouts will increase, you'll find it harder and harder to discuss your problem, and your drinking will become bolstered with excuses. As I said earlier in this chapter about the 'I'll never do it again' syndrome, you'll experience persistent remorse as your efforts to control your drinking fail repeatedly.

You may find that your mood-swings are becoming more aggressive and grandiose. On going through this decline, you see that the pattern you are in can only get worse. By this time your promises and resolutions are already failing, you'll be losing interest in other things, there'll be work and money troubles, you'll be eating poorly, and you'll lack willpower. Gone will be the days of having any control over whether you will or won't drink: it'll now be a case of having to. Your tolerance for alcohol will decrease, and then you'll move into the phase of physical deterioration. Remember, alcohol is not a health drink. It's not going to improve your physical well-being or enhance your looks in any way. Continual use of alcohol will impair your thinking, and can lead in many cases to mental damage.

So, with this information, it would seem sensible to look at the options you have with your drinking.

The first option is to continue as you are; it is then likely that you'll experience the above consequences. Another option is to attempt to control your drinking. I use the word 'attempt' because that's probably what you have been doing up until this point. Trying to control something that you've become dependent on is immensely frustrating and soul-destroying, because once you've got the taste for alcohol, once you've had that first drink, you'll want another one and another one and another one. One is not enough, and thirty is not too many. Trying to control something that is becoming increasingly out of control is practically impossible, but I suppose it has to be acknowledged as an option.

You can most certainly try controlling, or cutting down, your drinking – though I am sure you have tried it already – but, as the chapter title says, it's not the amount you're drinking, it's the wanting to drink that's the problem, and if you're introducing this substance into your body then that wanting will be kept alive and the craving will continue. It's rather like throwing petrol on to a fire – alcohol ignites the need for more alcohol, and so the fire is never put out.

The healthiest option I know is abstinence. Before you start swearing at me or throw the book away, let's talk about this.

The word 'abstinence' doesn't just mean not drinking: it encompasses a whole range of behaviour. The first thing for you to do is to have an honest look at or make a list of what is going to happen if you do stop drinking. Let me ask you a few simple questions:

1　Is it going to cost you more money if you stop drinking?

2　Are you going to lose your job because you stop drinking?

3　Are you going to lose your driving licence because you stop drinking?

4　Are you going to lose your marriage or your relationship, or the respect of your children/friends/employer/employees if you stop drinking?

5　Are you going to keep falling over because you've stopped drinking?

6　Is your thinking going to be impaired as a result?

7　Are you going to continue to suffer memory blackouts and feelings of guilt because you're not drinking?

8　Are you going to lose your sense of humour and never laugh again, and be a miserable, boring person because you've stopped drinking?

9　Are you never going to play sport again or have any other interests because you've stopped drinking?

10　Are you going to love less because you've stopped drinking?

The answer to all these questions is 'No.'

Abstinence from alcohol means abstinence from all the

consequences you've been experiencing. Imagine for a moment what that one sentence means. It means your getting back some self-respect in your life and some control over your actions. More importantly, you will have a healthy future without being surrounded by all those indefinable fears. Imagine a day without telling lies and making excuses. Imagine a day free of wanting that next drink. If all this sounds like too tall an order, just remember that you're not quitting drinking everything: you're just quitting drinking alcohol.

Let's not rush into things too quickly. Let's move on to the next chapter so that I can give you some more identification and information about what's happening in your life.

4 When excuses have become lies

When people aren't worried about their drinking, there's no
need for them to make up excuses, let alone tell lies – lies about
whether they've been drinking or whether they've not; about
whether they stopped at the pub on the way home from work for
a drink after a hard day, or whether they stopped at the off-
licence to bring a few cans of beer home or a bottle of wine. If
there's no problem, then there's no problem telling the truth.
But if something's wrong, then all sorts of things start to happen.

When I talk to people I work with, I describe the following
scenario. It's just before 9.00 a.m. and a man is on his way to
work. He gets into a lift and meets a friend from the same
office. On the way to the tenth floor, the friend says, 'God!
Your breath smells as if you've been drinking.' The man says,
'Yes. I've just seen a couple of friends who're getting married
today. Unfortunately I can't make their wedding because I've
got too much on, so we had a couple of glasses of wine to
celebrate their great day and their future happiness.'

That's OK. It's being said by someone who doesn't have a
problem, who doesn't mind admitting he had a couple of
drinks because his friends are getting married. It's legitimate,
so there's no need to make excuses or tell lies.

Let's go back to the same lift, but the man who gets in *has* got a problem with alcohol, and he doesn't want anyone to know that he's been drinking on his way to work. It's sad, really, because the same friend will get in the lift, and the man with the problem will be sucking peppermints until he reaches the tenth floor because he doesn't want his friend to know he's been drinking. He will also be acting unfriendly so as not to have to speak, just in case he's caught out. It's silly, but it's also sad because he's trapped.

What can you say when someone confronts you with 'Why are you drinking at this time in the morning?' 'Well, I'm sick of drinking coffee'? 'I'm fed up with drinking tea'? 'I just thought I'd have a few large scotches'? It's not acceptable behaviour, and it really isn't good for you. A denial mechanism is creating itself around you, and you don't want to say what you've been doing.

There's one thing that you really do need to have when you constantly make excuses and tell lies, and that's a very good memory. The more excuses you make, the more lies you tell, the more you're building a web around yourself, and if you forget then people will notice.

The first feeling you have when you get caught out is anger, and you'll express that anger. You'll say to people, 'Get off my back!' Why don't they leave you alone? What are they talking about? But inside you know it's not right, and you'll ask yourself, 'Why am I doing this? Why do I have to behave like this? Why am I telling these lies?'

If it was easy to answer that and to put things right, this would be a very short book indeed. But once the web of denial starts around your drinking, it's hard – but not impossible – to get out of it.

R. D. Laing wrote a wonderful poem which I think really depicts the word 'denial'. See what you think:

> *There must be something the matter with him*
>> *because he would not be acting as he does*
>>> *unless there was*
>> *therefore he is acting as he is*
>> *because there is something the matter with him*

> *He does not think there is anything the matter with him*
> *because*
>> *one of the things that is*
>> *the matter with him*
>> *is that he does not think that there is anything*
>> *the matter with him*
> *therefore*
>> *we have to help him realize that,*
>> *the fact that he does not think there is anything*
>> *the matter with him*
>> *is one of the things that is*
>> *the matter with him*

Alcohol creates an illusion. It seems to put all your problems on hold. It makes you relax, and takes all your stresses and strains away. But as your web of denial becomes larger, it becomes increasingly difficult for you to realize how many excuses and lies are being told, because you're behaving in a way in which you don't think you are.

When people say to you, 'Why are you doing this? Why did you say that you were there when you weren't?', you'll retort with, 'I didn't say I was there. I didn't say that at all. What do you mean, "Why am I behaving like this?" Behaving like what? What's the problem? You're always going on at me. Why don't you leave me alone? Why can't you let me relax and enjoy myself like everyone else?'

But you're not like everyone else, are you? Everyone else isn't running around making up excuses and telling lies.

Do you feel good when you behave like that? I'm sure you don't. I didn't. Ask yourself this question: did you make as many excuses and tell so many lies before you started drinking? Think back, and be really honest with yourself. Did you really behave like this? I doubt it. All of a sudden you seem to be trapped in the dishonesty. If they only knew how you felt . . . But you can't tell them, because one of the things that's happened is that it's become increasingly difficult to talk about how you're really feeling, because you're continually talking about how you're *not* feeling: how you're not feeling trapped and as if you can't have a drink; how you don't feel that things are wrong around your drinking. You're talking all *around* yourself, rather than *about* yourself. I suppose it's like being Dr Jekyll and Mr Hyde.

This brings an awful feeling of isolation. The problem is that people are noticing it. They can see it, and you're trying to tell them that nothing's wrong when they can see that something *is* wrong.

It's easy for me to sit here as I'm writing this and say, 'It's like being trapped in a bottle,' but that's really what it is: you're trapped in a bottle, and you can't get a message out to let everyone know, because if you do then you'll have to say what's really been happening.

Can you identify with some of this? How are you feeling as you read this? Can you see what's happening? Do you realize how trapped you are in that bottle? As you'll have read earlier in the book, I was in it for years, so I know what it feels like and I know how you're feeling. I also know that you can get out of it. I know that you can break the pattern of the excuses and the lies.

Have a look back over the past week. Can you think how many excuses you've made because of your drinking? How many lies you've told? Think hard. Check that good memory of yours. You don't have to write this down – just think about it. Think of the occasions when you've made the excuses, or told lies to the people closest to you: your wife or husband, your boyfriend or girlfriend, your children, your mum or dad. Maybe you're on your own, in which case it'll be your employer or your friends. But most of all you're making the excuses to *yourself*. The person you're really lying to is yourself. You and I know that doesn't feel good, because it's going against the value system of the good, honest person you really are.

Another behaviour that goes hand in hand with this is feeling resentful. You'll feel resentful against the people you love, because they're getting very close to the truth of your drinking (or the truth behind your drinking that you don't want them to know). You'll be getting angry with them. You may even shout at them or get violent with them. You'll be behaving like you'd never have behaved before.

You need to ask yourself why this is happening to you. How can something that you love so much cause you so much hassle? How can something that you love so much make you behave like this? How can something that you love so much isolate you from people you love – even isolate you from your cat and your dog. Have you noticed recently how your cat or dog behaves when you walk in through the door? Animals can pick up the mood-swings as well. Sounds silly, doesn't it? Have a look next time. If your pet doesn't know who's coming home because of the mood-swings, how do you think the people that live with you feel? They're unsure of how you're going to behave; they're wondering what excuses and lies they'll hear from you tonight.

Is it OK to carry on like this? If it is, then go ahead – keep doing it. If it's not, then stop right now and think about how this is going to change, and how you're going to get out of this trap. How you're going to turn around and re-create that good, positive value system that you had. Look at how you're going to get honest again. There's only one way to do this, and that's by starting with *you*.

Before we go any further with this, has one person, or several people, ever spoken to you about:

- Your drinking?
- Your behaviour?
- What you do and don't do?
- What you should and shouldn't do, and what you should've done?
- How you should cut down, or how you should quit altogether?
- What you're doing to yourself and what you're doing to your family?
- How you're going to:
  - lose your job?
  - crash the car?
  - get knocked over by a car or a truck?
  - fall under a bus?
- Or how you're physically damaging yourself – you're shaking and have trembling hands, your eyes look awful, your skin looks dreadful, you're not doing your liver and kidneys any good, you're going to have a heart attack, you're putting on weight . . .?

Someone's probably spoken to you about all these things by now. None of this concern is worth *anything* unless you *need* to do something about the situation. I emphasize the word 'need'. It's not a question of wanting to do something. I know you don't want to give up something that you like doing so much (or think you like doing so much) and that you regard as social. If you've been hearing some of these things, though, then it doesn't sound as if you're being very sociable at all. Either way, *you*'ve got to realize that something has to change. It's no good if the wanting you to change only comes from other people.

I've said to some of my clients, 'You can get the Pope, the Archbishop of Canterbury, the Queen, Jesus Christ, plus me, plus whoever else you want, and we can all tell you that you need to do something about this and you need to change something, but if *you* don't feel the need to change, you won't.' So, as I say, the need to change has got to come from you.

You want to go on? You want to have a day of no excuses and not lying to yourself? Great! Make a plan for the day, and stick to it no matter what. See how honest you can be with yourself, and, remember, don't tell anyone about this – this one's for you.

Get a pen and write down a plan for the day (use the plan on page 54 as a basis). For example:

What do you want to do about your drinking today? Do you intend to drink? If so, make a plan of how much you're going to drink, and don't go over it. Make your decision. I'm not talking about how drunk you're going to get: take this seriously – this isn't something that we can joke about.

What time is the first drink going to be? If you're thinking of not drinking as much, then there'll be some time left over. Maybe you can use it to do something else, something you haven't done for a long time. Do you have some hobbies besides drinking? Go to the cinema or to the theatre. Go out for a meal. Take the dog for a walk (that'll make a change). Maybe you can do something with the children. Just get some sort of outline for the day. If you're working, well there's the best part of the day taken up. Have you started to drink at work? Let's see if you don't today. If you're going to have a drink on the way home from work, then make it the *one* drink. Make your plan, and stick to it.

If you start making a plan for each day, doing things differently and not making excuses or lying to yourself, then of course you won't be making excuses or lying to other people.

Just watch the reaction from other people. They'll notice it right away. If you carry on with this, the changes will start to happen. You won't have to keep covering your tracks with lies and excuses and continually feel bad about yourself. You'll very quickly stop deluding yourself and consequently start to feel better about yourself. This will also be a very personal affirmation: that you *can* be honest with yourself; that you *can* do something about the way you've been behaving.

The benefits are certain. As I said, the first benefit you'll see is the reaction of those around you – whether it's family, friends, employees or even the dog! Watch the reaction and

YOUR PLAN

Date

Today I have decided to:
[see page 52]

Please be specific; and remember, it's your choice whether you tell anyone else.

If you can't *consistently* stick to your plan, don't despair but learn from this experience. I'll help you later on with this.

Would you like to plan anything else for this day?

Remember, it must be something you choose. (Look at page 53 for some suggestions I've made if you're stuck.)

How did it go?

Anything you want to do differently tomorrow?

the way people start to behave towards you. You'll see a very positive change. People will enquire and want to know what's happening, because it's positive; or maybe they'll keep quiet in the hope that it'll continue. If that's the case, then that will let you know how much they really want you to do something about this.

Well done. Remember: this is all for you. But everyone else will reap the benefits too, and they'll change towards you. All of a sudden you'll not be met with negative comments, or people telling you what you should and shouldn't do – you'll be rid of what's been provoking you, of what's been making you angry and resentful.

In this healthier frame of mind, you may want to start thinking about what your drinking has been doing to you and to those around you. Who knows? – you may even start to believe that you need to quit completely.

5 Can I change? Of course you can

Of course you can change, if you decide to. But if you're deciding to make emotional and behavioural changes, it's important to ask yourself a few questions:

1 What does change mean?
2 What are you changing from?
3 Are you worth changing for?
4 Will you enjoy the changes you make?

Let's look at question 1: 'What does change mean?' Change means doing something differently: approaching a problem, a situation, a behaviour, a feeling in a different way, so that the outcome of this change will have a positive effect on your everyday living. Above all, change means making a commitment to yourself, and sticking to it no matter how hard it turns out to be. This is a discipline that you'll very quickly fall into, mainly because you'll see the benefits straight away. I've never met anyone who abuses alcohol that deep down inside doesn't want to stop doing it, mainly because the changes the alcohol induces in the person's behaviour make the person uncomfortable with themselves.

So really what I'm talking about is making changes around

the alcohol, so that the person that you really are will shine through. You're not creating these mood-swings on your own: the alcohol creates the changes in your behaviour.

If someone close to you is saying that you behave like Jekyll and Hyde, think for a minute. Is this before you've had a drink or after you've had a drink? I suspect it'll be after you've had a drink, because the alcohol will change your mood. Your mood becomes out of your control, which is very frightening, because that says that you can't do anything while you're under the influence of alcohol other than what the alcohol makes you do.

Ask yourself how many times, when you've been sober, you've said to yourself, 'I won't drive the car when I've had a drink.' Yet when you've had a drink (or drinks), you do drive the car. How many times have you said, 'I won't pick on my husband/wife/children when I've had a drink,' and look what you end up doing. How many times have you said, 'I'll just have a couple,' but that's always turned out to be a couple more than you said you'd have.

Are you getting the picture? No matter how much you promise or commit to yourself that it won't happen again, when you drink it does happen again.

I *believe* you when you say that you really were intending to have just a couple of drinks, because that's what I used to do, but it never works out as intended, does it? So what does change mean? Well, judging by this we've got a pretty good idea of what change means when you drink, and it doesn't seem to be a very attractive picture. So let's get honest with each other for a few minutes, and move on to that second question: 'What are you changing from?'

Are you happy with:

- the way you are when you drink?
- the way alcohol makes you feel?
- your control over how much you drink?
- the way you treat people around you?
- your insane and strange behaviour?
- your loss of memory?
- your blackouts?
- the seemingly destructive behaviour against yourself and others?
- the accidents, or near accidents, caused by your drinking?
- the other dangerous situations caused by alcohol?
- the physical effect that alcohol has on you?

You can deny all these consequences to other people around you, but this is between you and me. What are you changing from? What's so awfully hard to let go of? Judging by what we've just been talking about, most people would want to move instantly away from that behaviour. So what are you waiting for? What's the difficulty? Are you frightened that you can't make the changes? Is it because you've tried so many times before and it's always ended up the same way – that you always do exactly what you didn't set out to do? This time can be different. This time doesn't have to be the same as all those other times, because this time you actually want to make some changes in your life.

Look at the way you've survived so far. Is survival good enough? Is this the way you want it to be? Is this as good as it's going to get? Is this all you're worth? What's happened to the person who was going to make something of his or her life? What's happened to the person with the ambition and drive? What are you doing with all that talent that you've got? Are you going to keep it locked away so that no one else can see, hear or enjoy it? Don't you think that's selfish and sad? Maybe it's because you don't think you're worth it – which takes me to question 3: 'Are you worth changing for?'

Well of course you are! Of course you're worth good things! Why wouldn't you be? I don't care what you've done, you deserve better than this. You deserve to get out of this trap. The people around you also deserve better than this. The people that love you deserve better. If you don't believe that you can do it, let me believe it for you. Let me give you some affirmation. Getting this far in the book tells me that you're brave enough to take a look at yourself, that you're willing enough to hear some things you don't want to hear, and that you're being honest enough to ask yourself, 'Is this all I'm worth?' None of this is easy, so the very fact that you've got this far tells me that you've got what it takes to make the changes, and that you're worth making the changes for. Which takes me to question 4: 'Will you enjoy the changes you make?'

Well, if you don't, you can always go back to how it was. In fact that choice will always be there for you. But I doubt very much that, after you've made some positive changes in your behaviour, you'll ever want to go back to how it was. The reason I have the faith to say this to you is because I've watched so many people decide to make the changes that they needed to make about their alcohol. I've watched them really enjoy the benefits from making that decision.

Of course there'll be a part of you that'll say, 'Oh you don't have to bother. This is all a load of nonsense. You can carry on the way you are. It isn't as bad as you think. Don't listen to other people.' You'll especially hear those messages when you're craving for a drink, and all the bad times then won't feel so bad because you'll be telling yourself that everything's OK so that you can have another drink. But you know as well as I do that the bad times won't have changed if you have that drink. They didn't change before, so why would it be any different now? You need to watch out for that side of you that gives you those really negative messages and wants to sabotage your making any changes whatsoever, let alone enjoying them.

So the simple answer to the question 'Will you enjoy the changes you make?' is *yes*. In fact you'll enjoy them so much that you'll want to go on making them. The important changes that you'll make will be moves towards freedom, away from the darkness and despair that you've been living in. You don't have to take my word for that. I asked some people that I've worked with to write about a day in the life of their drinking and what it was like for them. I'd like you to read these stories from people who've really been in the depths of despair with their drinking but have made a decision to come back and make positive changes to lead a normal life.

While reading these stories you may think, 'But I'm not as bad as this. I haven't had these consequences. I haven't done these things.' Add a 'yet' to the things you haven't done, because if you look back over your drinking you'll see how it's progressed this far, and there's no reason why you won't carry on going downhill if we don't make some changes.

Sam's story

He didn't want to open his eyes. 'Where am I?' he thought. 'It doesn't smell like a police cell. At least that's something.' Reluctantly he opened his eyes. Grey light was filtering through an uncurtained window. 'Is it early morning or early evening?' he thought. He'd pawned his watch a few weeks ago, so he'd nothing to tell the time by. He felt cold; he needed a drink. He was lying fully clothed on the floor of a small room with a single blanket covering him. There was a cupboard in one corner and nothing else. He suddenly realized he was in the back room of a friend's place, but he couldn't remember how he'd got there. The thought of his first wife came into his head. He tried to dismiss it. He felt lonely and fearful. He needed a drink.

'Is that a bottle near the fireplace?' he wondered. He rose

painfully and picked up the bottle. It was an empty cheap-sherry bottle. His head was swimming and he felt dizzy. His tongue felt like cooked liver. He carried the bottle through to the kitchen and filled it with water. His hand was shaking, and the bottle rattled under the tap. He was feeling really weak, and he made his way back to the room. He sat under the blanket and gulped down some of the water. The empty fireplace was surrounded with cigarette butts, so he picked out the longest one and lit it. Immediately his stomach began to heave. He had no time to get to the bathroom before spewing up the water. He continued gagging and retching on an empty stomach.

When the heaves had subsided, he went through his pockets to see if he had any money: he really needed a drink. He found £1.02 – 'Enough for a can of lager,' he thought – 'great!' He went back through to his friend's room to look at the alarm clock. It was 7.30. His friend was snoring on the sofa. He realized it must be morning, and the nearest shop with an off-licence didn't open until 8.30 a.m.

Returning to the back room, he lay down under the blanket, shivering, shaking and sweating, and feeling as if his heart was going to jump out of his mouth. 'God!' he thought. 'I haven't even got the strength to walk to the shop.' Finally, when he judged that enough time had passed, he went out of the front door feeling light-headed and disorientated. The pavement seemed to be undulating. There appeared to be smoke before his eyes. The walk to the shop was only a couple of hundred yards, but it seemed interminable.

He walked into the shop and, with rising panic, managed to slip two cans of lager into his overcoat pocket. He picked up a third can and paid for it at the counter with trembling hands. He walked slowly out of the shop, but once outside he quickened his pace.

When he got back to the house, he went straight to the back room and opened the first can. He was irritated by the froth which got between him and the strong lager. To begin with he took small sips, to prevent nausea; then he started to gulp it. By the time he had finished the second can and had started on the third, his shakes had subsided. His hands were steady enough to make a roll-up from the cigarette butts around the fireplace. His stomach started to feel warm, and the heaving cramps had gone. He felt that he could begin to think straight, but he was going to need some more alcohol soon.

He could hear his friend moving around next door. 'He got his giro yesterday,' he thought, 'so I could go and ask him to lend me a fiver.' His friend said, 'OK,' and with the fiver he returned to the corner shop and bought a quarter-bottle of vodka. He then caught a bus into town. By the time the bus had reached town he'd finished the vodka and was ready to do some begging. He begged in the underpass for about an hour and a half and got enough to buy a big, cheap bottle of wine from the supermarket nearby. He returned to his pitch and was relieved to find that nobody else had taken it. He drank the wine and begged for another couple of hours. By that time he'd got enough to buy himself a couple of pints at the pub. He started to feel more cheerful.

In the pub, he saw a couple of his friends and some other cronies. They drank until his friends had to go back to work. They'd bought most of the drinks. 'How am I going to carry on drinking?' he thought. 'What am I going to do for the rest of the day? I'll have to steal from somewhere.'

He went back to the supermarket and walked around and around, and when he was sure there was no one looking he took a couple of bottles of whisky and stuck them inside his coat. He picked up a newspaper from the magazine rack and walked to the checkout. He began to feel really uncomfortable and started sweating. He could feel his heart pounding inside his coat. 'Oh God, I hope no one stops me. I hope no one's noticed.' He started to shake. He thought he was going to drop the whisky. He was sure that people could hear the bottles banging together because he was shaking so much. 'Thank God the checkout lady doesn't seem to take much notice.' In fact she didn't even look at him, and he felt invisible. 'Has it come to this?' he thought. 'Do I look that bad?' 'Yes you do,' another voice in his head said. He held out his hands for the change. His hands were dirty; his fingernails were filthy. 'It wasn't always like this,' he thought. Then he quickly dismissed those memories from his head.

He walked quickly from the supermarket and made his way back to his room (if you could call it that – he lived in a dosshouse). He opened the only cupboard in the room and found some capsules which he'd got from a doctor in one of his failed attempts to control his drinking. He swallowed three of them with the first gulp of whisky, then continued drinking. Inevitably he thought about his wife. He was lonely. He began weeping, then sobbing. He remembered no more; he drank himself into oblivion.

And that's where Sam stayed until he made his decision, until he'd lost pretty much everything in his life. He decided that something had to change, that he was going to stop drinking. He didn't know how; all he knew was that there had to be something better, and that he was worth living for. It was hard work for him, but he made it. He asked for help, he took the advice, and he made the changes that were necessary for him to make a comeback and be a person again. For quite a few years he was a 'human doing' instead of a 'human being'. Today he is a very changed man and is successful in his life, and he has managed to put that nightmare behind him, a day at a time.

You don't have to go as far down as he did, or as I did for that matter. If your present situation is uncomfortable enough for you, then now's the time to do something about it. This is the time to make your decision and to make some changes. Can you change?

Michael's story

He woke up at first light suffering from dehydration and guilt in equal parts. He never could work out which was the worse of the two, but on thinking about it the dehydration could be cured – with another drink. The guilt couldn't be cured, because he hadn't yet come to know how to change.

The first task was to find his glasses. This was not as easy as you might think. He always placed them as near as possible to him, wherever he might be, and that was important, because he never knew if he was going to wake up at home or in somebody else's home or wherever. When he located his glasses, he could see Ruth in the bed next to him, and he knew he'd made it home.

So he sneaked out of bed and up to the stacked books on the floor. He found the remains of a bottle behind them, and drank some, then he just made it to the toilet in time to throw up. Throwing-up was something he'd got used to, because he'd had ulcers, and he'd had a very bad stomach. Nothing at all to do with his drinking of course – he just had a bad stomach. Despite that, he came back in and drank some more to replace what he'd just thrown up. Then he tried to climb back into bed without waking Ruth, without waking more of the guilt. He lay there, shivering and pretending that he was asleep, until she got up resignedly and got ready for work.

Her brother called to pick her up for work, and she shouted goodbye rather loudly into the flat to make sure her brother knew that Michael was home, because her brother worried for her and she tried to keep up appearances. She did this to the extent that she often shouted goodbye to an empty flat in the mornings to make her brother think that Michael was there, going to work and deluding herself that he was at home so that she could get through another day.

That's what the beginnings of their days were like.

As soon as she'd gone he galvanized himself, because needs must when the devil drives, and the devil in the bottle drove him. He took a bus to town and got there by 9.00 a.m. The pubs opened at 10.30 a.m. where he lived, but he went down a back alley and in a side door, and presented himself rather well (so he thought). He passed the time of day with the landlord, ingratiating himself – not only getting an early drink but getting it on credit.

After about fifteen minutes, Joe came into the bar. Joe was looking for an early drink in order to get the courage to go and face the tax man, so Michael took up his usual role and appointed himself Joe's tax adviser – for a fee of course. By 10.00 a.m. the deal was concluded and he now had £10 in his pocket: his fee from Joe. By 10.30 a.m. the pub was legitimately open and the regular customers were coming in. For a while Michael was beginning to feel no pain and was beginning to jolly up a bit as he went into the morning.

About an hour later it was time for a change of scene, and off he went to the pub across the road. In a zigzag pattern, he worked his way towards the centre of town, never missing a pub unless, of course, it happened to be one of the ones he was barred from – and he didn't like to think about those too much. Invariably it was the landlord's fault: they were all bastards. He had to try to keep his wits about him going down the streets, because in the small community where he lived there was a likelihood of running into people to whom he owed money – maybe money for a job that he'd promised to do, been paid for in advance, but had never done; or money owed to someone to whom he'd subcontracted out work that he wasn't capable of doing himself, then drinking the money when it came in and never paying the person who'd done the work. These were fairly regular events. Apart from the embarrassment, he knew that this wasn't how he wanted to live, it wasn't how he wanted to be known by people, it wasn't how he wanted to behave; but the drink was more important than anything else.

By mid afternoon he found himself in the company of a bunch of hard-drinking navvy subcontractors. This was the kind of company he liked, because he could impress them with what little knowledge he'd picked up in his life. He'd been fortunate enough to get a slightly better education than them, and he took full advantage of that. They were also impressed that he could do the work they could and that he had no hesitation in fighting alongside them and living the life that they generally lived. He hid very successfully from them the fact that he did it out of sheer desperation: he hated every minute of it, and fear ran his life for the most part. The fear of being seen to be afraid was probably the biggest single fear, and that was what kept driving him on to prove that he was as good as the next person, though he didn't really believe that to be true.

The session continued on into the evening. Some of the people were drifting away, because, although they could be described as heavy social drinkers, they didn't have his total obsession with alcohol. By about 7.00 p.m. he was left with the hard core: the people he was most comfortable with. These were the people who would excuse and justify any excess, because they were in the same boat as he was, and none of them could see that it was rapidly sinking. So they all struggled manfully or not so manfully to stay afloat together.

At 8.00 p.m. there was a phone call from Ruth, and he told the barman to tell her that he wasn't there. He then moved pubs, in case she came to look for him. He tried hard not to think about the way he treated people who cared about him, but he didn't quite make it, so he drank some more.

At 9.30 p.m. he woke suddenly with a start in another pub, not quite remembering how he'd got there. The pub around him was buzzing with people out for an evening's social drinking, and it was hard for him to fit in with a crowd like this, because he'd already been drinking for more than twelve hours at this stage. He found their happiness an irritant; he found their good humour difficult to cope with. He had nothing to be good-humoured about, so when he stumbled to the bar and knocked somebody's drink over he immediately took the aggressive role. Rather than apologize, he blamed the man for getting in his way. That was the way of it. That was constantly the way of it. When the man whose drink had been spilled took offence, Michael threatened him. As he had a bad reputation for violence, the other man backed off immediately, and for the moment Michael felt good about being able to 'handle' himself. Deep down, the truth of it was that this behaviour was as unacceptable to him as to the other people. The guilt resurfaced and wouldn't go away, so he drank some more.

At 10.00 p.m. he began to worry about the pubs closing, so he went off to one of the clubs. The club was a run-down, shabby affair with run-down, shabby customers and run-down, shabby staff. He knew all that because he'd worked there as well as drunk there. He knew that the steward at the club was on the fiddle, so he quietly blackmailed him into giving him free drink which he passed off as being on credit. Both knew it would never be paid for. By then he was somehow getting a second wind, and someone came in and said there was a party up in town. He immediately got a bottle from the steward and invited himself along to the party that the others were going to.

Though his sensibilities were well blunted by drink by now, he was still able to register the look of distaste that passed across the hostess's face when she saw him. Who could blame her? Having this particular drunk turn up on your doorstep was not a pleasant experience for most of the people in that small community, unless you happened to be a fellow alcoholic – then you could put up with near enough anyone, as he knew well himself. Other people, who didn't share his disease, knew they were in the company of a moody, unpredictable and sometimes violent person who was also unrelentingly morbid at this stage. The fun seemed to have gone out of the drinking some time ago, and now there was nothing left but loneliness and pain which he usually assuaged by attacking other people. The attack would often be simply verbal, but he was quite capable of doing as much damage with his tongue as he could with his hands, and he was aware of often being allowed into such parties not because he was welcome but because the hosts were afraid to turn him away. So in he went.

It took no more than a minute to register a woman at the other end of the room who shared his drinking habits and with whom he'd previously had a brief affair. So he headed straight towards her, knowing that she'd not reproach him for the amount he'd drunk already, nor for the amount he intended to consume in the immediate future. She was genuinely glad to see him – probably for much the same reasons – so for the next couple of hours they bullshitted each other, telling lies about what great times they'd been having recently. In fact they couldn't remember too much about any times they'd been having 'recently', and if they could and if they were being absolutely truthful they'd almost certainly have had to acknowledge them as being barely endurable, never mind great. They talked about who'd got locked up recently, who'd got in trouble, who was sleeping with whom, who was behaving badly – anything at all to keep the focus off what they were really doing with their own lives and how awful they'd become. It was a strangely comfortable moment in Michael's day, because at last he was with somebody whom he felt was in exactly the same place as he was, and with whom he could play this game wholeheartedly.

He must have fallen asleep again, because he came to with a start after about another hour, and she'd gone. The party was still in progress, but by now there were only a few die-hards left. He had an overwhelming urge to throw up, and he made it to the bathroom only just in time. It must've been the fifth time he'd thrown up today, but he'd stopped counting a long time ago; he'd normalized all this long before. So, back to the party and yet another drink, and suddenly he disappeared again inside himself, blacked out or asleep.

He came to with somebody seeming to throw a bucket of water over him. He'd dropped a cigarette down the side of the chair and, when it had started burning, someone had taken action. His first reaction was to hit the person with the bucket of water, and this he did – it wasn't safe being a good Samaritan around this guy. At that point the owner of the flat asked him to leave, at which he immediately took umbrage. He became very abusive, but did eventually go. He'd managed to hide a bottle in his jacket pocket, so he didn't leave empty-handed.

By now it was the early hours of the morning, and he thought briefly about going home, but decided that he was too drunk to walk. He lived a fair distance from the town and had no money for a taxi, so he'd visit the girl whom he'd been talking to earlier to see if she'd give him a bed for the night . . .

From this point on the day seemed to vanish, the night seemed to vanish. He didn't know if he'd drunk any more or not, or if he went to bed with the woman or not, because everything disappeared in blackout. This, by then, was a merciful release.

Today, Michael's story is very different. He is sober, happy and helping people in a way he would never have thought possible six years ago.

Joan's story

It was Wednesday morning, and Joan hadn't been to work since the previous Friday. She'd called in sick on Monday and hadn't bothered to ring at all on Tuesday. When she got up at 7.30 a.m. her head ached and her mouth was dry, but the worst feeling was in the pit of her stomach – that empty, hollow feeling. Within a few seconds of waking up, some memory of what she'd done the previous day came back, but she shut that down quickly, because she preferred not to think about what'd happened. Today would be different. She'd go to work and make a bigger effort, because she was becoming aware of the way people felt about her at work. They'd been supportive enough for a while, but now they were beginning to become impatient. She'd catch those side-long looks occasionally, as if to say, 'This woman's not coping. What are we going to do?'

She went into the kitchen, thinking that she'd make some breakfast, but as soon as she opened the fridge she felt waves of nausea, so she shut it again quickly. She felt a tremor throughout her body, and she knew that if she wanted to get out of the house she'd have to have just one small drink. She poured herself a small measure of brandy and drank it very slowly. The feelings of nausea passed; her body started to feel warm. Without thinking, she swallowed a couple of tranquillizers and drank some more brandy. She managed a cup of coffee and got dressed, and went out into the cold.

By the time she got to work, that morning's brandy and pills had caught up with yesterday's. She felt muzzy, and people seemed to be a long way away – their voices indistinct, their faces slightly blurred.

Her boss asked her a question, and she obviously didn't reply – although she didn't remember not replying – because she was asked the question again. She gave some kind of answer, but it clearly wasn't very satisfactory. They were sitting in the boardroom, in yet another one of those emergency meetings to look at possible redundancies. The room started to grow quiet, and people shifted uncomfortably. She wondered why. Then the talking resumed and she was able to let her mind wander as it had been doing before. If only things could change. If only her husband hadn't left. If only she could get the family home back. If only she wasn't having to live in that rather cramped, isolated little flat in an area of London that she didn't even like. If only she had some money.

Somehow she got through to lunchtime, and her workmate asked her if she'd like to go out and have lunch with him – just the two of them. Although this wasn't unusual, she felt uneasy about it. They sat in a quiet alcove in a little Italian restaurant, and Paul started talking about himself, his own family problems, his heavy drinking. Joan tried to say the right thing, tried to be helpful, tried to listen, but everything seemed disconnected. She noticed her hand was shaking slightly as she poured herself a large glass of wine. At 3.30 p.m. Paul said that it was time to go, and then casually asked Joan what was the matter. Joan talked a little bit about her own marriage, but that started Paul off again and he resumed talking about his. They were on their way back to work when Joan said that she needed to stop off at a shop, and they parted company.

Joan went into the nearest pub and had a couple of whiskies. By this time she was feeling quietly drunk and rather desperate. For the rest of the afternoon at work she tried to keep away from people as much as possible, but when it came to 5.30 p.m. she didn't feel like leaving. What was there to go home to? An empty flat, and an attempt to cook a meal which she knew she probably wouldn't bother with. Sometimes she and Paul would go back to the same restaurant and sit there for the evening, but Paul had something on tonight.

Joan found various excuses for hanging around at work, but eventually she ran out of them, and at 6.45 p.m. she made her way home. She thought of stopping off at the pub, but she didn't really like pubs, so it was better to go home – there was plenty to drink there if she wanted it. On the tube, she was aware of people edging away from her slightly. Her breath must have smelt very strongly. She fell asleep and woke up three stops beyond her own. A sudden and irrational wave of anger swept over her, but what was the use of it? Nobody knew. Nobody cared. Nobody cared a fuck.

She eventually got home at 8.30 p.m. and wished that she hadn't. She sat there, and the silence of the place enveloped her. She thought she might ring her children, and then wave upon wave of self-pity engulfed her. She felt the tears coming up, but her eyes stayed dry. She poured herself a large whisky, and reached for the pillbox. She didn't even attempt to make herself a meal: she knew that she wouldn't eat it. Sometimes the food would just sit there on the plate, sometimes she would give up halfway; usually she would throw it in the bin. She knew as she was drinking her second glass of whisky that it was one too many, but she didn't care.

Two minutes later she was vomiting. She hadn't managed to reach the bathroom, and trails of vomit followed her, spattering her clothes, the carpet, even the walls, as she finally made it to the loo. She tried to clean herself up, but it wasn't a very successful attempt. She put on some music – Mahler. As the lights of the houses opposite went out one by one, she sat on and wished she had the courage to end it all. Then she thought about her children again and remembered that she'd promised to ring them tonight. Another broken promise. She took off her stinking clothes and went to bed. Tomorrow she'd clean herself up.

Not long after this, Joan did clean herself up. She is now the professional person she always wanted to be, and is making up for lost time with her children.

Mary's story

Mary wakes up on a sunny Saturday morning with a sinking feeling – like dread in the pit of her stomach. She imagines each empty minute of the long weekend ahead: no plans, no commitments, no friends. She crawls out of bed. Leaving the curtains closed, she walks through her neat, empty flat into the kitchen. She opens a window. Outside, the street is so quiet it almost frightens her. She supposes that everyone must belong to a happy family that goes shopping on Saturdays, leaving no sound but her own to keep her company. 'Rather them than me,' she mutters under her breath.

She looks in the fridge at her large bottle of wine. She smiles. A calm, warm wave seems to roll through her out of nowhere. She can always have a glass of wine. She remembers her father's voice calling to her fondly, 'Want a glass of wine?' Suddenly everything feels all right again for a moment, and she makes some tea. She wonders how to fill the hours that must pass before she has earned a drink. She hasn't had a drink all week, and it was a difficult week: her first week at her new job.

Tonight is Saturday night, and she can do whatever she likes. As she eats her breakfast (a small bowl of cereal), she makes a list of chores: washing, ironing, cleaning, shopping . . . Her mind begins to drift off. She thinks of the week just gone. She didn't like her boss, who was bossy, disrespectful, unpredictable. Rude, actually.

'I've only been there a week and she's already telling me how to do my own work. If she knows best, why can't she type everything herself?' Mary begins to feel a hot flush of anger inside. 'I bet she's a spinster. I bet she lives all alone in Hampstead with some fussed-over cat and nobody talks to her. Serves her bloody well right.'

Mary catches sight of herself in the mirror: a pinched, sour face – the face behind her public face of smiles and charm and happy helpfulness. 'I'm like two people,' she thinks, 'and I don't like either of them.' She suddenly finds herself at the fridge again, gazing at her bottle of wine, when the telephone rings. She hesitates, but does not answer it. She listens to a friendly message from her sister as it tapes on to her machine. Mary stands stock still, staring into space. She can't see anything. Everything in the here and now is in a haze.

In her mind she runs through the next fifty years. She sees herself alone, unloved and unlovable, her face hard and sour, old before its time, still waking up to the silence at weekends after an unfulfilling week at work. She sees herself at Christmases and birthdays, always the odd one out, unpartnered, while her pretty sister kisses her children goodnight. She imagines poverty, illness, terrible misfortune, all endured alone, with no one to care about her. She feels herself a burden wherever she goes.

Woken from her reverie by the flashing red light on her answering-machine, Mary feels a great lurch in her gut – a sense of terrible foreboding about the rest of her life. She feels as though each little triumph will always be crushed by the outside world.

Her triumph had been that she hadn't had a drink all week. She'd left her job for a better-paid one. Her sister had phoned with her news that she was pregnant and her husband sent his love to his spinster-in-law. She hates them suddenly. She hates everyone. She feels cheated by them all. She thinks of her bottle of wine, her wine, her reliable friend, her cool bottle of wine. She races into the kitchen to the fridge and seizes it by the neck, but it slips out of her hand and smashes to the floor.

'No!' she cries. Her heart is racing with fear. She has to block out these terrible images of what tomorrow might bring; she has to extinguish them all as they rage about inside.

She clambers into the crumbled heap of yesterday's clothes on the floor, grabs her handbag and rushes out of the house. In the quiet street outside, she's like a madwoman steaming along the pavement towards the off-licence. On her arrival, she finds it still closed and curses under her breath before racing on towards the supermarket. 'That has to be open,' she mutters, brushing so fiercely against an old woman that she knocks her off-balance.

In the supermarket she jumps up and down with impatience at the end of the queue, sighing irritably as an old man fumbles for the right money to buy himself a loaf of bread.

The effective way to stop drinking

Mary has bought a five-litre box of white wine, because it seems more economical and less likely to break on her kitchen floor. She bursts through her front door and runs to the kitchen. She pours herself a glass of wine and knocks it back in one go. She fills the glass again, and drinks more slowly – even finding time to add a little ice.

She feels her fear subside as the hole in her guts subsides. She looks at her list of chores, and laughs as she tosses it into the bin. She lights herself a cigarette and sinks into her armchair in front of the television. She feels all right again. She knows she'll feel bad tomorrow – maybe even tonight – but now she feels all right. All is well again. She breathes out a sigh of relief.

'Wouldn't it be nice to have a husband and kids with me now, to watch television and to just be with me?' But in their absence she pours herself a third glass of wine.

Hopefully Mary will soon decide to seek the help that she so badly needs.

6 You're not a bad person

> Have a look at a photograph of yourself when you were very
> young. Look at that innocent little face. Ask yourself: did you
> want this? Did you want to turn out like this? Did you want to
> behave like this? Is this how you thought your life was going to
> be? Is this the way you thought you'd end up?

I imagine the answer to all those questions is 'No,' and I'm
convinced that when you started drinking you had absolutely
no idea of the effect that alcohol would have on you: that
you'd become so dependent, or hooked on it, or whatever you
want to call it. What about your dreams and ambitions?
Somehow they seem to have been left to one side. You just go
round in circles. Things don't change for the better: they
just seem to get worse.

I think it's very important at this stage for me to help you
separate your behaviour when you're drinking from your
behaviour when you're not. For example, when you're not
drinking, would you do the sorts of things that we've been
talking about? Would you behave like that sober? I doubt it.
It seems that you only behave strangely, or do the things you

wouldn't normally do, when you're drinking. Consequently, when you sober up or have time to reflect on what happened the last time you were drunk, you feel bad. You feel as if you're a bad person, but you're not. It's the alcohol that provokes the negative change in you. It's the alcohol that seems to take away your values, turning you into another person who behaves in a way that's alien to the real you. When you're under the influence of alcohol, you don't have any choice in what's happening.

Look back at the diagram on page 30. Can you start to identify the mood-swings? Are you still going from normal to positive, or can you see what happens now when you drink? You're moving more towards the left and starting to experience different feelings, and the more negative feelings bring about negative behaviour. Can you see the difference, with what used to be a very social thing for you to do now bringing very antisocial consequences? Can you identify yourself in the diagram with the excuses, the rationalizations, the blaming, the externalizing, the minimizing that you use as defences around you? Can you start to visualize the vicious circle that you're trapped inside that I've been talking about? Can you see the need to break out of that?

Let me give you an assignment to help you see what I mean:

Write a list of character assets that you have.

Let's examine them. Have those character assets been mentioned to you recently, or are people now saying to you, quite frequently, that you *used* to be the following?

- So kind
- Punctual
- Caring
- Fastidious
- Reliable
- Friendly
- Willing to help
- Conscientious
- Selfless
- Nice to be with
- A fun person
- Talented
- Creative
- Warm
- Gentle
- Safe
- Trustworthy
- Someone I could tell my troubles to

What else are people saying to you? What changes and concerns are people expressing to you? Be honest and write a list of what's being said, and compare it with what used to be said.

How do you account for these changes? What's happened? Do you think this is anything to do with your drinking? Would you like to be once more how people used to describe you? Would you like those sorts of affirmations?

Let's have a look at your belief system. How strongly have you felt about the following in the past?

1 Drinking and driving
Can you remember denouncing people who did this? Can you remember looking in a newspaper and seeing that a child or an old woman had been knocked down, and the driver had been drunk? Can you remember saying how awful that was and what a waste of a life, because someone had been driving a car while under the influence of alcohol?

2 Telling lies
Can you remember when this wasn't such a major feature of your behaviour? When it wasn't such a necessary thing for you to keep doing? Can you remember how you felt when other people told you lies, you knew they were telling lies, and yet they continued to do it? Can you remember saying, 'Gosh, I wonder what's wrong with him. I wonder why he keeps doing that'?

3 Taking alcohol from other people's houses without asking
Has anyone ever come to your house and helped themselves without asking you? Have you ever had a feeling that somebody was coming around to your place just to get a drink, rather than

coming to see you? How did that make you feel? How would it make you feel if someone treated you like this?

4 Being unfaithful and promiscuous
Is it OK to behave like this while you're in a relationship? Is it acceptable, especially these days, to put somebody you love at risk?

5 Lying about how much you're spending on alcohol
How long has this been going on, and why tell lies if your spending on alcohol is not a problem?

6 Losing interest in your job when it used to be one of the most important things in your life
Once you were conscientious, and it was important for you to achieve.

So, again, how do you account for these changes? What's been happening? Are these things taking place in your life because you've consciously decided that they will?

I doubt whether you'd want to change your value system so dramatically. I doubt that you'd want to behave like this. Why would you? What's the pay-off from this sort of behaviour? As I said earlier, you're just going to continue feeling bad and remorseful about the way you're behaving, and this will isolate you more and more from the people you love.

When you're asked about your behaviour, or confronted

about a particular situation, it becomes increasingly harder to explain it away. The excuses are harder to find, and you've made them before. All the time you're doing this, internally you're feeling more and more disgusted with yourself, because this is going against the grain of what you really believe in, and so you're bound to feel bad.

What I'm saying to you is that you're not a bad person. You're not a liar, a thief or a cheat, or a manipulative person. You're someone who's getting caught up in a web of behaviour that doesn't belong to you, and doesn't even suit you. Again, ask yourself the question: 'If I wasn't drinking, would all this be happening?' I think the answer to that is clear, but you've got to decide whether what's happening is getting bad enough for you to do something about it.

We're up to Chapter 6 in this book, and you've had a lot of information. You're still with me and you're still reading, so that tells me that you're identifying with this. One of the important facts to hold on to if you're going to make some changes is that what's happening to you does not reveal the person that you truly are. It seems that when you drink you can't be responsible for your actions – which is frightening in itself, because we're talking about you being totally powerless and unmanageable when you have that first drink. You can't guarantee what's going to happen or how you'll behave, or the outcome of any situation. Think about that for a minute. How does that make you feel? Does that sound like social drinking? If it does, then I think you'd better get a dictionary and look up the definition of the word 'social'. I don't think its definition includes any of the consequences I've been talking about. You and I may have to very quickly get a hold on what's happening here, because the longer this goes on the harder it is to get out of, and there's no knowing what might happen in the meantime. I'm not saying you can't get out of it: what I'm saying is you need to start thinking about how much you're in it, to break away from the denial that surrounds a lot of this behaviour, because if you don't think there's anything wrong then you're not going to do anything about what everyone else is telling you is wrong. You're not going to see things the way they're seeing them.

I suppose one way of facing up to that is to ask yourself whether you think that people close to you, who love you and worry about your well-being, would be telling you lies? That they'd be making up fabrications about your behaviour? Would they do that? Of course they wouldn't. They're worried. They're watching the deterioration of someone whom they love. In lots of ways so are you, but it's difficult to admit. The only way that you're going to make a start on this is by taking a look at what's happening to you and around you, and asking yourself, 'Is this what I want? Is this what I need? Is this giving me happiness in my life?' Is this what the little boy or girl in the photo wanted for themselves? Is this what they dreamed about? Was this their ambition? Was this what they wanted to attain in their life?

It might sound as if I'm being hard on you, but I'm not. The main purpose of this book is to help you realize what's happening, and to guide you out of the web of behaviour that you're weaving for yourself: to get you out of the trap of being a bad person and back to being the good person you really are.

7 The love affair

Have you ever thought of your drinking in terms of an affair? A real, serious affair?

Let me help you a little bit. Can you remember the first time you fell in love? Your first date? Your schoolboy/schoolgirl crush? Can you remember how difficult it was to think about anything else, and how important that person was to you? How upset you felt when something got in the way of your having a good time in your relationship, or when something went wrong? That person was the most important thing in your day, and you wanted to be with him or her as much as possible.

In lots of ways this seems to be happening with your drinking. A lot of things in your life are now being pushed into second, third, fourth or fifth place. Your drinking stays on the top of the list. We have to look at the 'love affair' you're having with alcohol, and what that affair is costing you emotionally.

What comes first? You? Your family? Your children? Your job? Wife? Husband? Hobbies? . . . Or your drinking?

If it's your drinking, then something's wrong, because the

other things I mentioned are an important part of your everyday life and an important part of people's value systems. Alcohol doesn't usually fit into that category, and especially doesn't come at the top of the list. I say that alcohol doesn't *usually* fit into that category, but if it's a problem and there's a serious preoccupation with it then it *will* be at the top of the list.

So what's the price you're paying for this? Well, if alcohol is more important or is *becoming* more important than anything else, there'll be lots of problems: the people around you (your wife/husband, children, friends and employees) will not be happy. They're being pushed into second or third place because of your obsession with drinking.

Ask yourself: would you like to be put into second place? Would you like to be the little boy who wanted to play football or wanted help to put his train set together? Would you like it if you were the little girl who wanted her mum to spend some time with her and give her much-needed attention? When alcohol comes first, none of these 'normal' things happen, and your wife/husband/children go uncared for and don't get love or attention.

I wonder how your employer feels when he's paying you a good wage and you're not getting the job done. That hardly makes good business sense. People *want* something, and if you're busy having an affair with alcohol, all they'll get is alcohol-related behaviour. That doesn't make for a good employer-employee relationship.

One of the hardest parts of the affair is your preoccupation with it. From the time you wake in the morning, it's never out of your mind. You may say, 'But I'm not drinking in the morning,' but that doesn't matter – that alcoholics necessarily drink in the morning is one of the myths of alcohol that I'll talk about later in the book. It doesn't matter if you're not drinking in the morning at the moment, because you may be thinking about drinking. You may be clock-watching for the time you can go to the pub, or for the time you can nip to your locker where you've got a drink. Maybe you've got alcohol in your car, or in your office drawer.

You may be preoccupied with waiting for the day to end, when you'll get that long-deserved drink. Put an 's' on the end of 'drink' – make it *'drinks'*. If you're only having one drink then there isn't a problem, is there? But it's the little bit more than that, when that first drink leads to the next . . . to the next . . . to the next. Even if you don't plan it that way, that's the way it seems to be going.

Maybe your preoccupation is, 'Where's my next drink going to come from, and what have I got to do to get it?' That's not an unfamiliar feeling for many people. You may be thinking about how you can cajole or manipulate your way into getting into a position to have your next drink.

Of course, there's all the boring business of disguising that you're drinking – having to mask the smell of your breath; having to walk that bit straighter and watch your words; deciding where you can say that you've been, even though you haven't been there. Remember what I said in Chapter 4 about needing a good memory for making excuses and telling lies? How about driving your car after you've had these drinks? Maybe that'll start to tell you how serious your affair is: you're willing to endanger the lives of other people while you're driving under the influence of alcohol.

It's so lonely, isn't it? It has to be lonely. 'Two's company; three's a crowd' – you know the old saying. There's you and your alcohol – who else do you need? Who else do you want? So you're also becoming the *lonely* drinker. There's a deep-down feeling of loneliness that stays there even though you drink a lot. It never really goes away. Next time you're in a bar, or wherever you drink, look around and notice how many lonely drinkers there are.

I can't paint a complete picture of what's happening to you, so, if I'm missing out some bits, you need to put in the rest. But I'm sure you realize by now that you're not drinking like everyone else. You don't seem to be getting many of the 'social' effects of drinking, because to get them you need to be sociable in other ways for most of the day, and if you're not drinking most of the day then you're preoccupied with the thought of it.

So what does all this mean? Simply it means that there's more denial, both to yourself and to those around you.

The people around you are noticing this. This love affair, this total preoccupation, does not go unnoticed by other people. Yet if you're in a state of protecting your drinking then you'll obviously deny it. That makes things even more crazy. Let's face it: people with healthy love affairs don't deny them, do they?

This sort of behaviour can only lead to you and your love ending up very, very alone together. It's a no-win situation, because you can't *talk* to alcohol. You can't *embrace* alcohol. You can't ask advice from it, and there's no lasting comfort or love coming back from it. All you're getting is that constant, nagging, lonely feeling.

Everyone around you is disagreeing with what you're doing. How many people do you know who hide their love affairs under the bed or in the garden shed, who dig holes in the garden to bury the love affair and then dig it up again, who hide it in their coat pockets or in their briefcases, under the sink, in teapots, in or on top of wardrobes, under cookers, behind fridges, in bathrooms and toilets? That's where alcohol is usually hidden when you don't want other people to know you're drinking.

Of course, there's always the other side to this: there are people whose attitude enables the affair to go on. There are people who find the way you behave funny and rather colourful. I'm often reminded of this story:

It's 10.30 a.m. and girls in an open-plan office are typing. There's a middle-aged woman at the front of the office. She's been there for a few years, and she's probably one of the most experienced typists in the office. She gets up to go to the toilet and takes her handbag with her. She looks a bit dishevelled and nervous, but she makes her way there. By this time most of the girls are looking at each other and nudging each other, smiling and laughing, because they know she's going to the toilet for a drink.

The woman goes to the toilet, opens her handbag, takes out her quarter- or half-bottle, and drinks the alcohol.

There's nothing loving about that is there? There's nothing sociable in that affair – just a lonely, middle-aged woman sitting in a toilet in the morning, drinking. Ask yourself: is that normal behaviour? I think not. Yet people laugh at her while she's killing herself, for she will kill herself like this if something doesn't change.

So there are people who will enable the affair, but I wouldn't term them as 'close friends' or 'good people to be around'.

Where are you in all of this?

- Are you preoccupied?
- Are you hiding and protecting your supply of alcohol?
- Are you putting you or alcohol first?
- Are you a lonely drinker?
- Are you getting more and more caught in the denial of your drinking?
- Are you getting the response that I've spoken about from the people around you?

- Are you starting to feel some physical effects? Your body isn't going to go unscathed, because constant alcohol abuse does no good at all to your kidneys, your heart, your liver and your central nervous system – at least I haven't seen it recommended for healthy living.

So what sort of an affair is this? Is it:

a) a *love* affair, or

b) a *bad* affair?

You need to ask yourself these questions. If you say that most of the things that I've talked about in this chapter haven't happened to you, put a *'yet'* at the end of that, because if some of them have then it's more than likely that the rest will follow. All of this can only end badly, unless you break off the affair first. If it's left to your lover, alcohol, it will take you down a long, dark road and leave you somewhere that you don't want to be. If you're unlucky enough, there won't be many people around to pick up the pieces.

That doesn't have to be the case at all. You can end this affair any time you wish by just putting down that glass, or putting down that bottle. You can be in total control of this. It's not as if you've got offspring from this love affair. But maybe you have! Maybe you've some bottle that's still unopened. Well, it's simple: don't open it – give it away. I doubt whether you'll break the bottle or pour the contents down the sink, but you could give it away.

What I'm really talking about is a *termination* of this affair, because it's leading you nowhere except places where you thought you'd never end up, to a state which you would've denied that you would ever reach. We're talking about a divorce, or even a trial separation. How about giving it a try? Or do you still want to go on down that dark road? If not, let's see how you can get off it.

I'll give you another short assignment:

Think about your preoccupation with alcohol:

- What time do you start thinking about it? How much in advance are you planning that next drink?
- Are you denying that you have alcohol in your home, or on your person, or in your office etc., when in fact you have?
- How often through the day are your thoughts taken up with alcohol? Do you find this preoccupation getting in the way of your everyday life?

Ask yourself how quickly you respond to an invitation where alcohol *is* involved and an invitation where alcohol *isn't* involved.

Ask yourself how many times in the day you're attempting to control your use of alcohol, perhaps starting off by saying, 'Well I'll just have one drink ... well maybe I'll have two – but no more,' then finding that you're having a lot more than you initially said you would.

Make a list of how many times you've been late during the last

---

few days, or maybe haven't turned up for appointments you'd previously arranged.

How often in the week have you been late coming home?

How often have you driven under the influence of alcohol?

Remember how many times you've said to yourself in the morning, 'It's not going to be the same today – I'm going to do something different.'

As we work through the book, you'll do various other assignments. Please keep looking at all of these, so that you can reflect on some of the situations we've been talking about. As the picture develops, you'll see the effect that your drinking is having on your life.

8 The house inside

The hardest thing to talk about is the way we feel – or at least it seems so. When I work with patients or clients, one of the first objectives I have is to try to help them explore their feelings, so maybe in this chapter that's what you and I can do.

What do we do with our feelings? Where do they go? When we express feelings, does that mean we don't have them any more – that they're over and done with? Maybe we don't express our feelings, but we bottle them up instead. Then what happens? Do we let other people define our feelings for us? Do we let them suggest that we feel a certain way, and just agree with them because we don't want an argument – we don't want to upset them, we want them to like us – or maybe because we just don't want to tell them the way we really do feel? Maybe we're hurt or afraid, feeling shameful, isolated, remorseful or sad. Maybe we can't trust other people enough to let them know how we're feeling.

There's so much involved in expressing our feelings, because there's a lot at stake. Once we *do* start to talk about and disclose how we're feeling, we're exposing ourselves. I suppose in some ways we're at the mercy of the listener and of what the listener may do with these disclosures. However I'm not talking about an everyday situation, like this:

'*Good morning, how are you today?*'

'*Oh, I'm fine.*'

Or the woman who walks into the shop and says:

'*Hello, Mrs Browne. How's everything at home?*'

'*Oh, it's OK. Everything's great. The garden's wonderful. The dog's fine. The birds are singing.*'

Or:

'*Hello, Mr Smith. How are you today?*'

'*Oh well, you know . . .*'

What does all that mean on a feeling level? Not a lot really, because those sorts of disclosures or expressions are very superficial. In lots of ways that's how people do interact with each other: on a very superficial level – 'Good morning', 'Good evening', 'Good afternoon', 'Good night', 'How are you?', 'Lovely weather', 'Shame about the weather.'

What I'd like to talk about is our *inner* feelings. Our deep feelings. Our important feelings. Feelings that really determine our moods. It's probably been said to you, 'Gosh, you're moody today.' What if that expression was changed to, 'Gosh, you're *feeling* today'? Think about that – what would it be like if someone said, 'You're really *feeling* today. Tell me about it'? What do you think you'd do? What do you think you'd say? One of your reactions might be, 'Don't be silly. Stop talking like that. What's wrong with you? You've been reading some silly book.'

So in most respects feelings aren't talked about. They're talked *around*. If people feel strongly about certain issues, they'll argue about them. Have you ever noticed what happens when people are arguing? Everyone speaks at once. How does anyone listen when everyone's speaking at once? Well, the answer to that is: nobody does listen. So how does anyone get heard? How does anyone express themselves? Well, they don't, and for people like you and me who have a lot of feelings and don't have the chance to talk about them, or to get some help with them, one of the ways to deal with this is to medicate our feelings.

That's what we do when we drink alcohol. There are certain feelings that we don't want to talk about, so we want to change them. So we have a drink. In fact the feelings don't change: I think what changes is the way we *express* our feelings.

Have you ever noticed what happens when you've been feeling angry but you've decided not to express the anger and have had a couple of drinks? Once the couple of drinks have started to work, you have some more drinks, and then your angry feelings come out in an unpleasant way. I don't think you'd have wanted to behave like that, but it's been taken out of your control because the alcohol has taken over – the alcohol is now in charge of your feelings and the way you express them.

It's like when you wake up in the morning and the first thought that comes into your head is, 'Oh I didn't, did I? Oh God, it must've been a bad dream.' But it wasn't. You did behave like that, and you're dreading seeing people because all of a sudden it's dawned on you what happened: how you behaved, how you expressed yourself. But that wasn't you – that was the alcohol, because the alcohol was in charge.

I often use the idea of a 'house inside'. We have an emotional house inside where we store our feelings, and it seems to me, through my experience of working with countless people, that we store our feelings in one place. We store all those feelings in a room and keep the door very firmly closed, and only we have the key or the combination to open that door. Sometimes we do open it – on our own, in the privacy of our inner selves. We go into that room and it's dark, because those feelings are dark, and it's frightening because there are so many of them. We very quickly shut the door again.

It's like when somebody comes to visit you and you're not expecting them. Your living-room's a bit untidy, so you lift up the cushions and put the newspapers underneath them, or you put stuff behind the sofa – you run around putting things out of sight. That's what we do. We store all these feelings away, and we forget about them. Then sometimes we feel depressed or strange or moody without knowing why, but basically it's because of all these unaddressed issues and feelings that we don't talk about or haven't been talking about.

If you want to clear out a drawer of old papers, you have to look through them, to see what you want to keep and what you don't. It's the same with our feelings: we have to explore them; we have to have a look at whether they belong to us or not – whether those feelings of shame, remorse, guilt, anger, sadness were given to us, or whether we really do *feel* like that. This is very important – in fact it's one of the keys to freedom within yourself. I cannot stress enough the importance of looking at our inner feelings and understanding how they affect us and our moods.

You may not have thought about any of this before, and that's OK: why would you? Generally people just go about their business and do as they do. But when you're doing something in your life that seems to be causing you distress and causing other people to show concern for you, then it's time to look at *why*. The quickest way to *why* is to look at your feelings and how you may be using alcohol as a cushion for a lot of emotional problems. And also at how alcohol can distort these feelings.

Have you ever noticed how much easier it is to become angry when you're drinking? Or how much easier it seems to be to be honest – or honest as you see it – when you're under the influence? In reality if you're on the receiving end of this anger, or of this so-called 'honesty', it's very threatening and extremely hurtful.

Remember how I talked earlier about how we want to change the way we feel? If you're constantly using alcohol, then your feelings will become caught up in the pattern of behaviour that alcohol causes. Remember, alcohol doesn't make things clearer; it distorts situations. It distorts perceptions. It distorts your hearing and your thinking. To simplify it: it makes mountains out of molehills.

Let's look at that fear that you seem to keep experiencing. A good friend of mine once said, 'Fear stands for "False Evidence Appearing Real".' I said, 'What do you mean?' She said, 'Well, Beechy, have you ever been asked to do something, maybe for the first time? Maybe to stand up in front of a lot of people and make a speech, or present a workshop, and you've been really nervous about it, and you've been dreaming about it. You've been preoccupied with it and you've gone through all the scenarios of failure: how people would walk out, or how they would boo, or how they would react in the worst possible way. The night before you gave the speech you didn't sleep. When you got to do whatever it was, you felt really panicky and nervous, but you got through it and did really well. None of the things that you'd feared had actually happened. Then all of a sudden you started to think, "What was I worried about anyway? What was all that fear about? Where did all that false evidence come from?" It appeared real because *we* create the fear.' We tell ourselves that we're not going to succeed, and immediately we get into feeling and believing that we won't. Alcohol is a way of reducing that fear, but with very negative consequences.

It's like wanting to tell someone that you feel annoyed with them, but you can't because you're frightened (for whatever reason). However, when you've had a few drinks, have you noticed what happens then? You certainly tell them how you feel, but it won't be in the way you really want. It'll come out angrily and distorted, and you won't feel good. You may *believe* that you feel good at the time, but when you sober up you definitely won't feel good about what's happened, and you'll have bigger difficulties with that person than you had originally.

If you could think of the same situation and deal with it soberly, it would be very different. Think about it. You'd still have that fear of 'What's going to happen?', but you wouldn't act in the same way. You have a right to feel, and a right to be yourself. You have a right to feel and express anger, and to be treated as an adult. It's also OK for you to make mistakes, and it's all right to change your mind. Why shouldn't it be OK to say that you don't agree, or you don't understand, or that you really don't care too much? You have a right to express your feelings, and you also have the capability of expressing them without alcohol. If you think back on past situations, you'll very quickly realize that you really don't convey how you're feeling.

It always seems so much easier to be angry, doesn't it? I see anger as being like a curtain – like the theatre curtains that part for the first act of a play to begin. Behind the curtain are all the feelings of shame. Lonely feelings, guilt projection, discontentment, discouragement, ambivalence, abandonment, defiance, despair, despondency, helplessness, gullibility, immense vulnerability and unending feelings of inadequacy – they're all there. Or anger is like a veil that prevents people seeing through to the feelings underneath.

It's easier to get angry than to deal with these other feelings, because then people won't see them – people won't experience how much pain you're really in, because anger keeps people away. Anger is the big message of, 'Leave me alone. I can handle it.' If only we realized when we behave like this that we're isolating ourselves more, and more, and more.

Remember how I spoke about alcohol acting like petrol thrown on to a fire? Not only does it ignite the need for more alcohol, it ignites the anger and the rage, and the feelings of isolation and loneliness. That dark room where you keep all those feelings suddenly becomes alive, but it's not a healthy life within those walls – it's tormented. There's no brightness or peace. There's no serenity, and the courage that you really have is lost in a maze of pain. Where has the playful and peaceful side of you gone? And your love, loyalty and empathy for other people? The encouragement you used to give: where's it gone? These qualities are being drowned. You're isolated from the positive, and connected to the negative.

'Why doesn't everyone who has a drink feel like this?' you

may ask. Well, quite simply, they don't because they're not made up like you and me. Only the small percentage of people who'll drink alcohol, use drugs or abuse food, or compulsively behave in some other way will feel like this. You can be jealous of the other people and be resentful of them, but you'll never be like them in this respect. But if you stop using alcohol you will stop the consequences that follow from your drinking. Your life will be up and down, because all life is up and down, but whatever it is that you're suffering now because of your drinking will cease. Don't pick up that drink, and it *won't* happen. It doesn't take an Einstein to understand that one, does it?

Just because you stop *drinking* doesn't mean you stop *feeling*. Learning to cope with the feelings you have is the key to staying sober and not having to resort to the crutch of alcohol to help you cope or to medicate those emotional storms that you experience. It is possible to live very happily without alcohol. It is possible to really enjoy yourself, even at a party, a wedding, a christening, at Christmas or Easter. At whatever occasion you choose to name, it is possible to enjoy yourself without using alcohol.

You'll experience the feeling of *freedom*: of being your own person, being out of the trap, being able to make a choice instead of feeling totally powerless and unmanageable. *You'll* be the boss over your own feelings and emotions. You'll be able to feel, and to *express* your feelings all the time – to feel the highs and the lows, the joy and the sorrow, the love and the pain. Basically you'll start to feel *reality*, and like a whole person – physically, mentally, emotionally, spiritually, socially. You'll start to develop the ability to maintain genuine relationships rather than relationships based on broken promises, or one-sided relationships as they have been in the past. You'll be able to love and be loved, and you'll be able to meet your needs without the need of alcohol.

Imagine that. Physically you'll have the ability to make the most of yourself, and you'll start to show care and respect for your body. You'll start to think very differently about clothes, how you look and how you feel about yourself. You'll start to eat differently and be good to yourself. That inner self-will won't be destructive – it'll be extremely positive. You'll have the ability to take responsibility for yourself: to choose to do or not to do; to follow through on your decisions and to finish what you set out to do; to achieve things and have values. Your mental ability will be enlarged. You'll learn to grow, to integrate, to change and especially to remember events and ideas in the past. Just think how difficult that's been. You'll be able to plan, to imagine and to have some positive dreams for the future rather than living in a daily nightmare.

Here's an assignment for you:

Look at the list of feelings below. Over the next few weeks, try to think about identifying how you are feeling and start to get more aware of these feelings and how they affect you. If you identify a lot of anger, then try to look behind that anger – that will really help you see how to deal with it more effectively.

Also look at the list of defences and do the same. Be honest with yourself and see how you act — see how you *feel*. Remember that feelings don't have to be negative — if they are, there is a way out, and that way out is by *doing* something about them.

Feelings

Abandoned	Adventurous	Afraid	Alone
Ambivalent	Angry	Anxious	Apathetic
Ashamed	Bewildered	Bored	Calm
Caring	Cheated	Cold	Concerned
Confident	Cowardly	Defeated	Defensive
Defiant	Discouraged	Down	Eager
Elated	Embarrassed	Energized	Envious
Excited	Failed	Fearful	Foolish
Frustrated	Grateful	Guilty	Happy
Helpless	Hesitant	Hopeless	Hostile
Hurt	Impatient	Inferior	Irrational
Jealous	Joyful	Kind	Lonely
Loving	Miserable	Natural	Nervous
Numb	Overcome	Overjoyed	Pained
Peaceful	Pious	Playful	Pleased
Proud	Provoked	Put out	Refreshed
Rejected	Reluctant	Remorseful	Resentful
Respectful	Secure	Selfish	Self-pitying
Snappy	Stubborn	Successful	Superior
Suspicious	Tired	Tranquil	Trapped
Understood	Unhappy	Unsure	Unworthy
Used	Warm	Weary	Worthy

Defences

Agreeing	Complying	Conforming	Disagreeing
Generalizing	'I don't know'	Justifying	Levity
Living 'in your head'		Making excuses	
Shifting	Silence	Verbosity	
Yes, but . . .			

9 Empty bottles, broken promises

I wonder how it would feel if the shoe was on the other foot
and someone continually promised you that a situation
wouldn't happen again: if, even though you'd heard the
promise before, you went along with it one more time, but
what you'd hoped *wouldn't* happen did happen and it was the
same old situation again. Would you not care? Would you not
be bothered, because you'd expected it to be that way? 'After
all, it's happened so many times before.' Or would you be
hurt? Hurt by the fact that every time the promise was made,
it was made with conviction and emotion? In fact it felt like
more than a promise: it felt like a commitment – a commitment
to you as an important person in the other person's life. Maybe
you'd feel betrayed, let down or even undervalued. Maybe in
future you'd just go along with a promise or commitment,
while knowing deep inside that it wouldn't be any different.

Think what it would be like to live with that on a daily basis.
How much trust would there be in the relationship? You
know the old rebuke, 'If you really loved me, you wouldn't do
this.' It seems that every time the promise of love is made, it's
broken again because there's something getting in the way.
There's something happening that causes this behaviour, and
that something is alcohol.

Alcohol probably causes more problems in relationships than any other substance, because so many other problems can evolve and be created by unsociable drinking. How can you have a relationship based on empty bottles and broken promises? Let's put the shoe back on the foot to which it belongs.

Think for a moment:

- When was the last time you *didn't* drink more than you planned?
- When was the last time you were home when you said you'd be?
- When was the last time you got a job done on time?
- When was the last time you did the things you promised yourself you'd do?

If, while you're reading this, you're thinking to yourself, 'But these situations only happen now and again,' there's still something to think about: alcohol's still causing you a problem. And it's a problem that isn't going to go away: it'll just get worse. Have you ever noticed how the broken promises always come in pairs – one before you have a drink, and one after you've finished? For example, 'I'm only going to have one drink,' or 'I'm only going to have two drinks.' Ask yourself: when was the last time you had just one drink, or stopped at two? Then, when you've finished the last glass, the second promise is made: 'I'll never do that again. I won't have another drink. It'll be different next time.'

Broken promises equal broken trust, and one of the things we always want people to do is to trust us. But how can they when we continually betray their trust? Try as you may, you continually do it. I'm not saying you're a liar, a cheat or a thief: all I'm saying is that, when you make promises around alcohol, they constantly seem to be broken. This means that the trust that people have in you will be destroyed. It goes beyond the family to employers: how can they depend on you? How can you be a trusted employee? How can you be given the responsibility to get the job done and be a role model? You're not meeting deadlines, you're falling behind in your work, and you may even have a record of time off with sordid illnesses and ailments which usually equal having had too much to drink. If you're an employer, what work rate will you get from your staff when they see you not keeping time, or not taking responsibility for what's supposed to be happening in the workplace? Broken promises also equal lack of respect, and if you're in a position of responsibility and you aren't meeting the expectations that people have of you, then there will be a lack of respect from those around you. So the effect of broken promises doesn't stop with the family: it will affect you in most areas of your life.

In what way is this affecting you? Well, you may say to someone, 'I promise I won't do that again. You can depend on me: that's the last time it will happen,' but even while you're saying this there's another voice in your head saying, 'This should keep them off my back. This should keep them quiet. This should do the trick.' It's ironic that, even though you know you're saying these things, you're thinking the opposite. How does that make you feel?

I can remember when I behaved like that. I felt very badly about myself. I felt like a cheat, especially when I was looking at the other person looking at me, and that person really wanted to believe me. I would even say to my children, 'I promise I'll play with you. Daddy will be there in a minute.' I never was. I never had any intention of being there with them, because the alcohol was becoming more important than they were. My wife tried to get me to look at the way my alcohol was affecting everything in our marriage, and I would say, 'Yes, I understand. I promise it won't happen again. I promise I'll do something about it,' yet I knew that I wouldn't. Deep down inside I used to feel like a fraud, a non-person.

Looking at that situation now, it's like looking at someone who couldn't make a decision, because he was totally power-less when he picked up that first drink, and who became unmanageable, because he couldn't *not* drink once he had started.

Every time you break a promise, you break a law within yourself. But, because of the trap with the alcohol, there doesn't seem to be any alternative. It's ironic that you still wake up with the same problems and worries, but with another broken promise to add to the list.

When I was in treatment for my drinking, I was in a family session with my then girlfriend, Josephine, who's now my wife. The counsellor who was taking the session asked about the promises that had been broken, and the times that I had said I would do things and yet I hadn't done them. She said, 'Can you remember any instances, Beechy, when you didn't do things?', and I answered very defensively with, 'Well, there may have been a couple of times, but really not many.' I was always pretty straight with her. Whereupon Josephine produced a portfolio – it looked like *War and Peace* – with detailed times and dates of things that I'd said I'd do and didn't do; times I said I'd be home and wasn't; times that I'd gone out saying I'd be back in half an hour, and came back two days later; promise after promise after promise that had been broken. To be honest, I couldn't remember them. I sat there dumbstruck. While Josephine read out those various instances, I got flashbacks of familiarity with what she was saying. I couldn't actually remember the situations, but they *felt* familiar and I knew that it was the truth. I sat motionless while Josephine continued to read out the broken promises. She became more upset and tearful, and I was frozen. The counsellor asked me how I was feeling, and I said I was numb. She said, 'Don't you have any emotion and feelings about what you're hearing?', and I honestly couldn't explain how I was feeling. It was as if a cloud had opened on top of me and I was being rained upon, but not with rain: with all the promises I'd made and had broken.

I'm sure that session with Arlene Kelman (the counsellor) and Josephine was one of the turning-points in my getting better, because the whole enormity of the lies and things that I'd said became very real to me then.

As I sit here in a garden with the sun shining down on me

writing this chapter, I feel really good that I don't have to make promises that I can't keep. At least today I have a choice in the promises I make, and at least I can fulfil them.

An ironic part of this for people like you and me is that we set out with the right intentions, but those intentions very quickly get lost in the effects of the alcohol. For example, when you say you're only going to have one drink, you may well mean that; but once you have one, you want another. Once you have that one, you have another one with that one; and when their effects start taking place then the whole scenario very quickly changes from what you initially set out to do. So, yes, I do agree if you say to me, 'But that's the way I started out – I really did mean what I said. My promise was valid, but then something else happened.' I know that something else happened, and this is really what I'm talking about. Every time you have more to drink than you said you would, something has happened that wasn't initially in the plan. This seems to indicate very strongly that you can't make a promise about what will or will not happen when you have a drink.

The effect of this behaviour on families or partners can be devastating. If you aren't in a relationship, you'll have people around you who care for you, and they'll be experiencing the same feelings of rejection, and it will cause them to worry. But I won't go on in too much detail about this here, because the next chapter is devoted entirely to the family.

If you're having difficulty identifying with this chapter, maybe it would be a good idea for you to sit down and make a list of the tasks you've set out to do and the promises you've made to yourself. (I'm not talking about promises that you've made while you've been drunk or drinking, because those promises are very rarely kept.) List the ones you've actually completed against the ones you haven't. Maybe then you could start thinking about the promises you've made to people close to you — your family, children, close friends. Then widen the scope again and look at the promises you've made to other people. Get a picture of what's been happening.

Make a summary chart of the promises you have kept and broken in one week, so that you can also visualize what we are talking about. This is how one of my charts looked during my drinking:

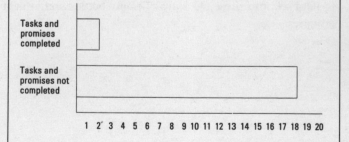

This showed me the chaos in my life as a result of my drinking.

After you've made your lists, look at the individual situations that you've written down and look for the pattern. Look at what has got in the way of you fulfilling those promises and tasks. If you can remember the excuses you made for breaking those promises, write those down too, and you'll start to get a picture of your behaviour. Please keep the lists that you make, because I think it's important that you keep each one of your different assignments for reference, so you can look back over the way you've been behaving, and hopefully see the change that's beginning to happen in your behaviour. It will be very useful for self-affirmation as to the progress you're making.

Remember, while you're reading through this book, you may be going to be making some major decisions about your alcohol intake, so it's very important to have some information to look at to affirm your future behaviour. It's very easy to fall back into those old ways of empty bottles and broken promises.

10 Family

This is one chapter in the book that you probably won't want to read, but you really need to. Unless you start to understand what's actually happening around you, there really won't be any overriding motivation to stop.

At least five people around you are affected by your drinking. These five people could easily be your boss, your employees or your friends, but more often than not they're your family.

You see, you're not alone in all this. You have a supporting cast. Maybe we can look at this like a play, a drama. This is pretty much the last act, and few people who abuse alcohol play out their drama alone. I think that, blind and unknowing, you take a whole cast of supporting characters down with you.

Everyone whose life touches yours is in one way or another affected by your drinking. It's easy for your boss to sack you, or it's easy for your employees to leave you. Your friends can drift away or say that they don't want to see you again, or that they don't want to invite you around any more until you start behaving a little bit differently. But what can your family do? They can't turn their backs so easily on someone they love. They choose the only alternative that they can see: to stay and adapt to the behaviour of your drinking.

I'm talking about your wife or your husband or your girlfriend or your boyfriend. If children are involved, they've no opportunity or choice at all – they've got to stay with whatever their mum or dad decides. That's really where the damage starts, because there's no healthy way to adapt to someone who's abusing alcohol.

I know this is going to be painful for you to read, and it'll bring up a lot of feelings, but we have to face the facts of what's actually happening around you.

The first thing that your family do is to devise a set of rules to protect you, while still trying to stop you from drinking. Crazy as this may sound, this is what your family have to do, because, remember, they don't really know what's going on, except that mum or dad's not behaving normally. So the family begin to accept the unacceptable.

The first rule about this unacceptable behaviour is that the drinker's use of alcohol is the most important thing in your family's life. While you're obsessed with maintaining your supply of alcohol, your family are obsessed with cutting it off. While you hide the bottles, your husband, wife or partner searches for them. While you stockpile, they pour the liquor down the sink.

But there's always more. An active drinker never really runs dry. There's always some way of getting another drink. There's always someone who'll buy you a drink. There's always money somewhere, only it may not be money that was meant to be spent on alcohol. It could be money for food or bills, or for your children's clothes and shoes. It could be money that's been kept for a rainy day (and not a wet day in a pub). If the family's money is being used like this, it shows the level of dependency: that alcohol is the most important thing in the drinker's life.

The drinker and the family become like two football teams: their goals lie in opposite directions, but they're all playing the same game. The drinker's use of alcohol is the overriding concern.

Rule 2 is about how your family deal with the shame of the alcohol abuse. The first thing the family say is that the cause of the family's problems isn't alcohol. They'll deny that you're abusing alcohol, and later they'll deny that you're *depending* on it. Why? Because of the shame. Families are systems, and they don't like telling other people what's happening in their system. They don't want the neighbours to know. But the neighbours will know, because if there are arguments they'll hear them. If you're staggering home late at night or driving the car erratically up the street and banging doors, they'll notice. They can't fail to notice, because it's abnormal behaviour. If your children are going to school with your neighbour's children, they'll say little things which will feed back to the parents. But the shame of all this is very threatening to your family. Your husband or wife doesn't want other people to know exactly what's happening. When alcohol dependency is finally staring them in the face, they'll deny that that's the root of the problem for which they're seeking help.

Isn't it funny how you treat the very people who are trying to protect you? Even though this protection is enabling for you, isn't it funny the way you shout and treat them as if they're your enemies?

When children are involved, especially young children, and they see their parents arguing all the time, with one parent going to the pub, drinking at home and being distant, what do you think they think? Of course, they think it's their fault: it must be something they're doing. This in turn affects every part of the children's lives.

Can you see what's happening? Can you see the way your behaviour filters right through the system of your family? Sometimes when I'm giving lectures to family members, I use the concept of the family as a central-heating system. You have the boiler, the thermostat and the radiators dotted around the house. If you think about it, the boiler is usually the father, the thermostat is the mother, who tries to keep the peace, and the radiators are the children. If the boiler goes out of commission, the thermostat is powerless and the radiators will be affected. If the thermostat goes out of commission, the boiler won't function properly and nor will the radiators.

Once there's alcohol abuse within it, a family can't function properly. The family may manage to function after a fashion, but only in a very dysfunctional way. Which takes me to rule 3: the family tries to rationalize what's really quite irrational.

According to the problem drinker, someone or something else always caused whatever difficulties there may be – the dependent person avoids his or her guilt by blaming someone else for the situation. The scapegoat could be the husband/wife, the children, the job, colleagues at work, the boss, the marriage – anyone or anything to get rid of the feelings of guilt and worthlessness.

Have you ever wondered what it's like for someone to be blamed for something they don't understand, that they can make no sense of? You see, your family take on your unacceptable behaviour, and at the same time try to rationalize it. But how can you rationalize an irrational situation? Quite simply, you can't. This leads to feelings of craziness, because your denial – the drinker's denial – has become so strong that you transfer all the guilt, shame and anger on to your family, and your family start to blame themselves.

So the behaviour advances until no one says what they're really feeling, which is rule 4. Everyone's treading on eggshells around you, and you're in so much emotional pain that you can't handle your family's painful feelings.

Imagine it's Friday night: your wife's at home with the children preparing supper. She doesn't know what time you're going to be home, but she hopes it'll be soon: that this won't be like every other Friday night, which in the last few weeks may have become the pattern for most other nights too. She starts to go through the same routine as before: she tells the children to go to their rooms, to be quiet, not to make too much noise and not to play music. 'Let daddy have his supper in peace, and don't ask him silly questions. If he wants to fall asleep, just let him do that, because you know what'll happen if you disturb him.' The fear is being set up before you even come home. 'Don't disturb him. Don't make any noise. Don't talk to him.' The *children* are getting these messages. What do you think they think? What else can they think except, 'Well, if we don't talk to him or make any noise, then everything'll be all right. So it must be our fault, and we must be the cause of all these arguments.' So no one gets to say what they're feeling.

It goes on, and on, and on, until the whole set-up is a total travesty of reality. Everyone's hoping that something's going to change, that one day you'll come straight home and it won't be the same story. But that doesn't happen. Little things become a big problem for you: getting out of bed, going to work or even sustaining a job, going to the shops. You're tired all the time. You're withdrawing deeper into yourself because of the guilt and the shame, and more guilt and more shame, until your family are looking at a shell – the remnant of what was once a healthy, strong and lovable person. Can you imagine what that's like – watching the self-destruction of someone you love? No matter how much you say things, no matter what you do, no matter how much you try to please or cover up for them or tell lies, nothing changes. It just gets worse. Can you imagine the pain that your family experience?

I suppose it's unrealistic of me to ask you that, but I think it's time to start thinking about it. If you don't start thinking about it and if there aren't some changes made, you're going to lose your family because they won't be able to put up with this sort of behaviour. If you're reading this and thinking, 'Well, I haven't done any of these things, I haven't caused any of these problems, I'm not behaving like this,' add a 'yet' on to that. You've come this far; what makes you think you're not going to go the whole distance if you don't make some changes?

When I talk about the pain of your family, I think back over the countless family sessions and groups in which I've been involved. One always sticks out in my memory. It concerned a very successful businessman who wanted some help with stress. He didn't think that there was anything wrong, other than that he was working too hard and that the stresses of his employment and the expectations put on him caused him to drink a little. Not a lot, but just a little. He ably batted back everything that I and the team tried to suggest to him.

We got his family in: his wife and three children. They also very ably batted everything back. They played by the family rules that I mentioned earlier: 'It's the stress of the job. What can we expect of him? He can't do any more than he's doing,' and it was everyone else's fault but his.

This continued for about three or four weeks. Then, in the middle of one of our group sessions, with about forty or fifty people, he turned to his wife and said, 'This is all a waste of time. I don't need any of this. I don't need to sit here in a group of people and talk about problems I haven't got. I'm a social drinker. It's stress I'm suffering from – nothing else.' While he was going on about how he hadn't got a problem, his youngest son, aged about six, got up from where he was sitting and moved between his elder brother and sister. The boy looked at me, and then at his parents. 'I've got something to say,' he said. To see this little chap sandwiching himself between his brother and sister made me think that he was going to take a risk, and a risk he did take.

The boy told his father that he had gone to the off-licence. Imagine a six-year-old looking up at the counter. He had said to the man behind the counter, 'Please don't sell my daddy any more alcohol, because he comes home and shouts at my mummy, and then he shouts at me, and then sometimes he hits my mummy, and sometimes he hits me.' You could touch the silence in the room. It was as if time stood still. The father and son looked at each other, and the mother looked down at the ground. The brother and sister were holding the boy's hands. The father's eyes filled up and he began to cry, and the little boy moved from his brother and sister to his father. I can assure you there was not a dry eye in that room. I must admit, for all the therapy and all the professionalism that we'd used, without that little boy's intervention his father would have probably continued with that behaviour, and destroyed himself and his family.

I'm happy to say that the man in question is now leading a very sober life, and has re-established his relationship with his wife and his family.

That is the story of just one of countless families who are suffering the unacceptable. Please hear what I'm saying: you're not the only one involved in this. If you're emotionally hurting, then your family are emotionally hurting with you. Why wouldn't they? They depend on you. They love you and care for you. Something's got to change. The secrets have got to stop, and the rules have got to be changed for healthier ones. Can the family survive? Yes it can, but the first step has got to come from you. You hold the key to the survival of your family, but you also hold the key to the destruction of your family. What I mean by that is this: if you're going to do something about your drinking, then you'll survive and so will your family. But if you're hell bent on the destruction of yourself, then your family, if they stay with you, will suffer the same fate. If there are going to be any changes made, they've got to start with you. You're at the top of the tree in this one, and you have the ability to change the rules that your family have set up.

At this stage of the game they need more than promises. They need to hear more than, 'That's the last time I'm ever going to have a drink. I'll never do it again. I'll quit tomorrow. I'll cut down. I'll change my drink. I'll stop drinking spirits. I'll start drinking wine.' Come on! How many times have you said that? If you're really honest, if you had a pound for every time you'd said those things you'd be looking at a reasonable amount of money. It's time for honest action and a positive change.

Do you love your family? Ask yourself that. Do you love them enough to take a step back and look at what's going on? If you feel as if you can't take a step back, then ask them. Maybe show them this. See if they identify with it. That's risky, isn't it? Is that asking for too much of a commitment? We're halfway through this book – we've got to get some action into the situation. You and I can debate until the cows come home. It's like talking politics in a pub: there's never any resolution – everyone gets to give their opinions but there's no change made, there's no progress. We're talking seriously about salvaging – or at least trying to salvage – your relationship.

If you're looking for a way to salvage your relationship with alcohol, then you'd better start reading another book, because I'm talking about what the real you wants, not what the addictive side of you wants. If you give in to that destructive side of you, you'll lose everything around you. For the people close to you, there'll be nothing for them to stay with: you won't be offering anything.

If you look back over what we've talked about, you can see the picture being painted. What are you actually offering your wife or your husband or your children? What are you offering them in terms of security and happiness and fulfilment and future? Don't put the book down – you've got this far, and we have to face the pain before we can get into some recovery. If you need to, read this chapter again. I've no wish for you to lose what I lost. Painful as all this is, it's also a very positive step forward in helping you to reunite yourself with your family and loved ones, whatever your relationship.

Family

With their love and support, you can break free, stop this daily torment that you live in, and move forward to the happiness and fulfilment in your life which you, your family and the people who love you so richly deserve.

It's your choice. If at this stage you don't think you've got any choices, then move on to the next chapter.

11 Making choices

If you had to choose between receiving a cheque for £10 or a cheque for £50, I'm sure you'd choose the cheque for £50: £50 goes further than £10.

Making choices about your alcohol consumption is quite simply the same as making other choices about what's best for you. We know that drinking too much is not good for you, physically or mentally, and trying to drink less than 'too much' may be proving difficult and so is causing you problems; or it may be that drinking by itself is causing problems and difficulties in your life. So making choices about alcohol comes down to making choices about something that's not good for you.

It's very important to have choices in our lives. There's nothing as bad as being told, 'Don't do this', 'Don't do that', 'You can't do this', 'You can't do that.' With most human beings, this usually arouses a rebellious instinct. If you tell a child not to do something, sometimes the child will do it anyway. I think children behave like that because they want to learn why they can't do something, or what will happen if they do. The same applies to your drinking.

Making choices

You will, by now, probably know the limitations surrounding your alcohol consumption. You may not want to accept these limitations, but that's not the issue: I'm saying that you will have learned them through consequences, reactions or comments from other people about your drinking. The choices I want to discuss with you in this chapter are those that you *need* to make, rather than those that you *want* to make. There's a lot of difference between wanting something and needing it. I have no desire to take your choices away from you, and I have no right or authority to do that. I just want to help you look at whether the choices you make are going to be healthy and fulfilling for your future.

The first choice you have is to stay as you are. If you're happy with your drinking, and the consequences when you drink, that's fine; but please don't think that reading this book is a waste of time. It's not. You'll probably have a friend, relative or someone close to you who's drinking too much, and you'll recognize their behaviour through reading this. So pass the book on to them.

If you're not happy with the way you're drinking and the consequences following from it, then you have the choice of doing something about it. In fact you have a number of choices:

1 You can choose to cut down your drinking.
2 You can choose not to drink every day or every evening.
3 You can choose to drink only at weekends.
4 You can choose to drink only during certain celebration

periods, such as Christmas, Easter, weddings, anniversaries, parties etc.

5 You can choose to stop drinking for a period of time to see how you benefit from that – in your health, for example, and behaviourally, financially and in your relationship with your family.

When you look at these choices, does it occur to you that there's something wrong? If you're convinced that your drinking is normal, sociable and just like everyone else's, then why do you want to make some changes? Surely you want to carry on the way you are? The fact is that you *cannot* continue; the time has come when you have to make some changes and make some choices.

I think it's great that you're willing to take some risks, and that you think enough about yourself to start looking at what you can do to make the quality of your life better. I support you 100 per cent in taking on this challenge, and so will the majority of people around you. They'll want you to make the right choices, because they'll benefit as well. If you don't like the choices you're making, you can always go back. You have the choice to do that too.

There's no need to start saying, 'I'll never drink again. That's it. I'll never drink as long as I live.' If alcohol is causing you problems and you wish to cut down, then quite simply cut down. You can't rehearse this; you've simply got to do it.

The concern I have about people attempting to cut down

their drinking, however, is that if they could have done it, they would have done it a long time ago. With a substance such as alcohol, it's easy to forget that it changes the way you feel. It changes your mood. It affects your thinking. So, as I've said in other chapters, you'll start out with the right intentions – 'I'll only have one or two' – but once you have that one or two you'll want more, because there'll be a change in the way you feel and you'll be in the early stages of enjoying that. Once you've had a certain amount of alcohol, you'll feel sleepy, or you may feel that you don't care any more. By the time you even start thinking about it, it'll be too late: you'll be drunk. So what's the point of trying to cut down? I personally think that if you have to think about cutting it *down*, you really have to think about cutting it *out*. If alcohol is the problem, then the problem is alcohol: stop drinking the alcohol and the problems surrounding the alcohol will stop. I know it's not easy, but who said it was?

I do know that the only choices you can make while you're under the influence of alcohol are:

- to drink more of it;
- to drive your car while you're under the influence of it;
- to behave in a way that you normally wouldn't;
- to talk to people in a way you never would while sober;
- to act more loudly and outrageously than you otherwise would;

and so on.

Making the choice not to drink alcohol a day at a time is probably the quickest way to see the benefits of this choice realized. There are only twenty-four hours in any one day – you'll probably be awake for sixteen of them, and work for eight of those sixteen; so, provided you're not drinking while you're at work, you only have eight hours to worry about! Just take it day by day, with no days off: this mode of thinking can be used for many different things, but it is especially effective for dealing with the misuse of alcohol.

Choosing to quit drinking may seem an enormous step, and it may be one that you do not readily want to take, but I think one of the best ways to approach this choice is to look at what *making* the choice will mean:

- How beneficial will that choice be to you?
- What will it mean in terms of money – i.e. how much are you spending to get these continued negative consequences?
- How much are you losing out emotionally by having such bad relationships with the people around you?
- How much more time are you going to have?

Make a list of the choices you'll have if you make the choice to quit alcohol. Think:

- How much time do you spend in the pub or at home drinking?
- How hard do you work, in order to spend the money you have, to feel how you feel?

If you're married, how will this choice affect the rest of your family? Will your children be disappointed to hear that you've stopped drinking? Will they be upset to know that you'll be home when you say you will, that you'll play with them, that you'll give them some attention, that you'll no longer shout at them for no reason? Will your wife be distraught because you're home on time, because you're eating the food she cooks, because you're able to hold a sensible conversation and share responsibility for the running of the family? Will she be upset that you're not driving your car while you're under the influence of alcohol? Or will your husband be upset to return home to a sober wife instead of someone who's incapable of cooking, looking after the children and running the house?

Please don't think I'm being flippant. Frankly, everything is going to change for you. Imagine not having all the hassles that go along with the (supposed) few drinks. The quality of your life will change 100 per cent. If you don't want that, then carry on as you are. However, I don't believe that you do want to carry on as you are. It's pointless for you and I to beat around the bush: we have to have a really honest look at what's happening in your life. I've no wish to waste the very valuable time that we have on this planet, but nor do I want to encourage you to continue your drinking, especially if you're having problems with it, because the next time you drink you never know what's going to happen. So now is as good a time as any to start making your choices.

The effective way to stop drinking

Make a list of the choices that you have if you're going to *continue* drinking, and another list of the choices you'll have if you are going to *stop*. I'll make a suggestion before you make your lists: ask yourself — what are you really giving up? If you're truly honest with yourself, I'm sure that you'll come to the right conclusion.

12 The magical myths of alcohol

I can remember having been at a treatment centre for my drinking for about three weeks. I was just coming out of the haze of withdrawals I'd been going through, and one of the counsellors said, 'We're going to watch a video this afternoon.' I'd no idea what it was going to be about or why it was going to be shown.

I sat down in the television room with the other patients, and the counsellor explained that the video was entitled *Guidelines*; it was by Father Joseph Martin – an American priest who was also a recovering alcoholic. The first thing that came into my head was, 'Oh no, I've got to watch a priest! I'll have to put up with a load of religion and he'll talk about God. What's that got to do with my stopping drinking?' I decided that I'd either close my eyes and doze, or pretend to watch the video but take no notice of it. I knew I couldn't get up and leave the room, because it was one of the expectations of the centre that you went to groups and watched the videos.

The video began, and a middle-aged priest with grey hair and a kindly face started talking. Within about a minute – if it took that long – I was laughing hysterically. I wasn't laughing *at* him, I was laughing *with* him, because the priest (Father

Martin) was telling jokes. The jokes were about drunks, and, although they were very funny, they were poignantly serious at the same time. I couldn't stop laughing, and tears rolled down my cheeks.

I'll never forget that, because it was one of the most significant times in my life – significant because it was the first time that I'd really, really laughed without a drink. I sat in that centre, having come out of the nightmare of withdrawals and DTs, and I laughed. It may sound strange, but the truth is that I'd never thought for half a minute that I could ever enjoy myself without alcohol. As far as I was concerned, if you didn't drink you were boring and miserable – a moron without any sort of life. 'What's life without a drink?' I used to think, and yet I laughed at a priest telling jokes.

For me that incident dispelled the first myth about alcohol. I found out that it was possible to laugh and have a good time without it. That was something I seriously thought I could never do.

I know this applies to a lot of people, because I hear it daily: 'What'll happen to me if I give up drinking? What am I going to do? I won't be able to go out! What's the point in watching the television without a drink ... or going to a party or wedding?' There are many myths surrounding alcohol, and in this chapter I'd like to go through a few of them with you.

By the way, one of the greatest pleasures in my recovery was meeting Father Martin, and telling him about that afternoon when I was in treatment – how I watched his video and how I found out that I could laugh without alcohol. He, being one of the most gentle men that I've met, sat and looked at me with tears in his eyes and said, 'Humour is so important in recovery. It's what helps people get better. If there isn't going to be humour in your life, then what's it all about?' He's right: if you're not going to be happy doing something, then don't do it. Maybe I shouldn't say this to you, but I'm going to anyway: if cutting down or giving up alcohol is going to make you so very miserable, then carry on drinking. I personally doubt that it will, as I think that if you're miserable it'll be because of a choice that you're making, rather than a condition that you're stuck with.

Back to the myths of alcohol. You've probably got a whole host of your own, so write a list of the myths that you believe about alcohol. Compare that list with some of the myths I'm going to talk about. You'll probably have quite a few that I don't discuss, so it'll be good for you to take a serious look at them and to come to your own conclusions.

One of the biggest myths, as I've already said, is:

1 *'I can't laugh without a drink.'*

How much laughing do you do while you're actually drinking? If you do laugh while you're drinking, how long does the laughter last before it turns into anger or remorse? I'm not saying that people don't have fun while they use alcohol – they do – but I'm talking about you and me. How much fun do *we* have? How much serious, good-humoured laughing do we do?

I used to laugh at the expense of other people while I was drinking – usually at someone's being incapable or prevented from doing something. How often do you laugh at the expense of other people? Is your humour nice humour, sarcastic humour, angry humour, or hearty laughing? I can honestly say that I've never had such a good time or laughed so much as since I quit drinking. I believe this is partly because I can remember in what situation and at what I've been laughing, even if it was a few days before. I can remember the joke and reflect on it without any haziness. I could never have done that before. Healthy humour is a big part of healthy living, and – believe me – *it* will be healthier as *you* get healthier.

Another great myth is:

2 *'Life would be dull without a drink.'*

Well, how bright is life *with* a drink? How much colour is there in your day, and how much are you enjoying yourself? Your life will be anything but dull without alcohol. Alcohol is a depressant: it anaesthetizes your feelings; it dulls your senses; it curtails your outlook. Take all that away, and life will be anything but dull.

Another favourite:

3 'I won't know how to spend my time.'

You'll be amazed at how much there is to do, and you'll wonder how you ever found time for your drinking. I don't want to start getting at you, but we have to be honest with each other. How about spending time with the people who are important to you – with your family and children? How about spending some time listening to your friends, who've spent so much of their time listening to you? How about giving some attention to yourself – to your well-being; to your health; to your body; to the things you've always wanted to do but have never found time to because you've been drinking? For once you'll actually enjoy having time. Time means that you'll have more choices, and choices give you a sense of freedom, and you'll have the time to enjoy that freedom.

4 'Alcohol relaxes me and gives me confidence.'

Well, I know it relaxes you – it relaxes you to the point that you pass out! It relaxes you to the point that you can't listen and you start slurring your words so much that you sound as if you're speaking another language. It's a myth that you need alcohol to give you confidence or 'Dutch courage'. You've already got confidence; you don't need alcohol to have that. You can do whatever you choose, and you can do it really well without the aid of alcohol.

5 *'Only tramps are alcoholics.'*

It's estimated that only 3 per cent of people with drinking problems live on the streets. I agree that many people who sleep in bus stations and beg in the streets abuse alcohol, but alcohol abuse has no social boundaries: it's everywhere. As I work in a treatment centre, I see people from all walks of life misusing and abusing alcohol, so I can assure you that all alcoholics are not tramps.

One prize-winning myth is:

6 *'All alcoholics drink in the mornings.'*

It doesn't matter what time you start to drink – it could be in the morning, in the afternoon, late in the evening or in the middle of the night – it's the wanting to drink and what happens when you start that counts.

7 *'I won't have a social life without alcohol.'*

I always find this funny, because I wonder how sociable you are while you're drinking. Speaking for myself, I used to get so sociable I couldn't speak! I'd fall over and be sick, and I'd be abusive and manipulative. So what's your definition of 'social drinking'? Of course you'll have a social life without alcohol – you'll have a wonderful one! Remember, you won't have stopped drinking: you'll just have stopped drinking alcohol. I guarantee that you can be much more sociable and socially-skilled without alcohol than with it.

8 *'I never have any fun without a drink.'*

This is a particular favourite. Taking that statement literally means that for most of your life you are miserable. How many hours of the day do you spend drinking? If you drink for only two hours of the day, are you going to be miserable for the other twenty-two? I doubt it. You'll have much more fun without alcohol. You're probably reading this thinking, 'It's all right for him – this is only what he says.' That's true, but there are countless people, like me, who are enjoying their lives without drinking. I guarantee it: you will have fun without alcohol.

9 *'I'll never meet new people if I stop drinking.'*

Why not? Look at it this way: when you go into a pub and you see the same people every night, how new are the people you're meeting then? Because you're going to cut down, or quit drinking, does that mean that you're not going to go out? Will you never be able to talk to people again? Of course you're going to meet new people. This myth really is a complete nonsense.

10 *'I can't go to parties if I stop drinking.'*

Does alcohol rule your life that much? Does it determine everything, even down to whether you can or can't go out? You'll find you'll enjoy parties a lot more, and in fact you'll be much better company than the majority of people who are drinking too much. You'll find that people will be interested in you because you're coherent, and because you're behaving how you normally behave without a drink. You'll actually enjoy yourself, and that'll really put that myth to rest.

Another myth that goes hand in hand with 'I can't go to parties' is:

11 'People will find me boring if I don't drink.'

Well, how interesting are you when you're drunk? I used to think that I was wonderfully interesting, funny and humorous while I was drinking. It was only when I stopped that people actually said to me, 'Thank God for that, Beechy! You were so boring and self-obsessed. You never listened or gave people the chance to give their opinions. As far as you were concerned, you were everything. You were the whole universe, and everything ran according to what you said.' I can assure you that that was the last thing I wanted to hear, but because so many people said it to me I had to start to listen to them.

Another contender:

12 'Everyone drinks, so I'll be the odd person out.'

You'll notice, if you really look, that many people don't drink, for various reasons. Maybe they don't want to be arrested for drunken driving, and they may feel that they have a responsibility to the other people on the roads. There are people who frankly aren't interested in alcohol – they may just have one or two drinks throughout the whole evening, and they won't be preoccupied and obsessed with it. Nowadays, more and more people are stopping drinking alcohol, as they're stopping smoking, because it's better for them. Drinking, like smoking, is becoming an antisocial thing to do. You won't be the odd one out, as there'll be many people not drinking, and you'll notice them.

A valid question to ask yourself is: who are you going to make these changes to your drinking for? I think that these changes need to start with you. You're the most important person in all this. You're going to get the benefits and rewards. People around you will also benefit as a result, but I think it's very important that the responsibility is taken by you, *for you*, because you're the one who's doing the drinking. So, remember, all this is for you.

One of the most startling revelations for me has been that I can now actually do all the things I ever dreamed of doing, within reason. I used to day-dream about many things while I was drinking, and now that I'm sober most of them have come true. I never thought that I'd get near them, let alone begin to realize them. So, for me, taking an honest look at the myths and challenging them has been an enormous help in my recovery, and I hope it will be a help to you too.

13 Keep doing what you're doing and you'll keep getting what you've got

I can remember the first time I heard the expression 'Keep doing what you're doing and you'll keep getting what you've got.' It was at a time in my life when I was trying very hard to control my drinking. In lots of ways it was a last-ditch attempt to prove that I could control it, so that I needn't try to control it any longer. Needless to say, every time I tried this, I failed – miserably. So this expression really niggled me, simply because I didn't want to admit that I couldn't control my drinking. I wanted to hold on to the belief that I was in charge of it. As you will have read earlier in the book, I was anything *but* in charge of my drinking. However, pride still remained with me, and the last thing I wanted to do was admit that every time I had a drink my life became totally un-manageable.

When you behave like this, you cannot be honest. I used to say that I *could* do something, when deep down inside of me I knew that I *couldn't*. There's a good example of honesty! It's all very well for me to say this with hindsight, but it's very difficult – in fact nearly impossible – to see this behaviour when you're so closely involved, because you're so busy defending yourself and trying to protect what you don't want to give up.

Before I go any further, you need to ask yourself if what you've got is what you want. If it is, fine. Keep doing what you've been doing and you'll keep getting what you've got. If you're not happy with what you've got, we have to look at how you can make some changes. The most effective way I know of doing this is to draw up a self-assessment of what's going on in your life. If alcohol is a predominating factor in your life, then let's have a look at that.

When I work with patients, I give them a self-assessment sheet. Filling this in is the first stage of acknowledging the power of the compulsion and the level of chaos caused by alcohol. In this chapter I've given you the responsibility of doing a self-assessment as an assignment. What you get out of the self-assessment will very much depend on how honest you are with *yourself*, because, as I've said before, this is for you. This isn't about anybody else, it's primarily about your behaviour with alcohol, so it's very important for you to take this seriously, and even more important that you're as honest as you can be.

As you and I haven't met, I'm not sure what stage you're at with your drinking, so I've had to set out this self-assessment a little differently than I normally would with patients I have in treatment. Let's have a look at the four main stages:

1 The early stage.
2 The middle stage.
3 The crucial stage.
4 The chronic stage.

All of these stages have equal importance, because they follow on from each other. If you think that, just because you're at a pre-problem stage, you won't move into phase 2, 3 or 4, be warned – they are interlinked with each other. Problems with alcohol follow a progressive pattern, and it's important that you and I separate social drinking from problem drinking. The distinction is quite simple: social drinkers don't have problems with their alcohol – they enjoy their use of it; they don't overdo it; it isn't taking over their lives; it isn't on their mind twenty-four hours a day; and neither will it be the end of their world if they don't have a drink. This isn't true for problem drinkers: problem drinkers have difficulties with alcohol both while they're drinking it and while they're not.

The pre-problem stage could, I suppose, be classified as 'social drinking', but somewhere along the way you cross that fine line where it isn't so social any more, where drinking seems to take on a greater importance in your life. Other people (such as husbands, wives, children) start to take a second place to the alcohol, as does your work. There's a marked increase in your alcohol consumption, and there'll be very noticeable changes in behaviour and in tolerance of people or situations that get in the way of your drinking, with angry outbursts when questioned about the time taken up with alcohol consumption. This is where the line is really crossed into the onset of a drinking problem.

There'll then be a marked dependence upon alcohol – an urgent need for the first drink. You'll take risks with alcohol, such as driving your car under the influence, putting your family in danger while drunk, working while under the influence of alcohol – dangerous in itself, whatever your profession may be. You'll have feelings of remorse and guilt about your drinking, but will be unable to express those feelings. Instead, you'll lie about your alcohol use. You'll start to plan drinking binges ahead of time, to have problems in remembering what happened while drunk (better known as memory blackouts), to experience noticeable mood-changes.

This takes us into the 'crucial stage'. Now you're unable to control the amount of alcohol consumed, saying, for example, 'I'm only going to have a couple of drinks' but ending up on a full-scale binge. Promises are always broken; all the old ex-cuses become more and more repetitive. Tantrums, angry outbursts, unrealistic resentments and expectations become more common. Personal hygiene is neglected; less and less effort is made with your personal appearance. Mealtimes are overlooked – you become undernourished. You feel sick in the mornings, possibly vomiting. You have tremors, your hands shake – it's getting to the stage where you can't even write your name. You have to drink alcohol in the morning to be able to face the day, and you continue to drink through-out the day to cope with routine situations. Eventually you're drinking all day and in a permanent state of intoxication. Your mood-swings are more unpredictable.

Now you're entering the 'chronic stage'. You're totally obses-sed with drinking. You've totally lost touch with the days and your feelings. You progressively abandon responsibility for your family. Your absenteeism and poor time-keeping at work increase and your work performance is poor. Relationships with colleagues or clients are disturbed. You have frequent accidents and minor illnesses. You deteriorate intellectually: your critical faculties and thought processes become progressively duller; discussion degenerates into stubborn arguments; you underachieve educationally, through apathy and poor concentration and memory. Financial dishonesty begins, with increasingly inadequate financial management. Progressive disregard for yourself and others results in gradual progressive disregard for the laws and customs of society. You deteriorate spiritually, with loss of hope, trust and faith in yourself and others. Further deterioration continues in all physical aspects – health and fitness. Memory blackouts increase still more. Life is a total preoccupation with alcohol.

These four phases have been researched and written about extensively by many leading people in the field of alcohol abuse, and the above descriptions are taken from many of these papers. As you can see, dependence on alcohol is a progressive pattern; however, its progress is not always in a straight line. Sometimes people with a drinking problem can become deluded into thinking that they are OK because they have stopped drinking for a few days or for a few weeks and their health and behaviour have taken a sudden turn for the better. It's very easy to fall into the trap of 'Oh, it's all OK now. Everything's fine. I've stopped, and it's all all right.' In fact as soon as the drinking starts again it's not all all right, and you don't go back to square one, you just get increasingly worse.

Once the dependency has got to this level, there is no controlling it. Unless help is asked for or an intervention is made, the consequences are horrific. So the importance of a self-assessment cannot be emphasized strongly enough. Again I have to say that if you're not going to be honest in this first-step self-assessment, then you're not going to reap the full rewards. It's important to take a look at what you've been doing and the way you've been behaving to get the full picture of how powerless and unmanageable you really are where alcohol is concerned.

If you're really willing to be honest with yourself, this will be the most important step you will take to help yourself with your drinking.

To do this self-assessment properly, it should take you about a week. That may seem a long time, but you need to think long and hard about the questions I'm going to ask you, and to write down (on separate pieces of paper) specific examples on each topic. When you have finished this, you will have a total picture of how your drinking has affected all aspects of your life.

To do the self-assessment *effectively*, you need to be specific in your answers to the questions, and give two to three examples for each answer. For example: when and where the situation happened, who else was involved, what your behaviour was like, how much you were drinking at the time. Take your time with each example. Think back and try to remember as best you can what the situation was and who else was involved. Be as thorough as you can. Remember, this is a *very important part* of looking at your drinking behaviour. It's the most important step you are going to take. Try not to exaggerate or minimize any of the situations you're going to write about. Try to answer the questions in numerical order and, remember, take your time. Don't rush. Get everything down, and then you'll see just what's been happening to you, and just how much alcohol is affecting your life.

If you then decide to stop doing what you're doing, you really will stop getting what you've got.

SELF-ASSESSMENT

In this assessment I want you to be *really honest* with yourself. Remember, this is for you – you don't have to show it to anyone.

Please answer the following with specific examples. Each example should state:

(a) When and where the situation happened.
(b) Who else was involved.
(c) What your behaviour was like.
(d) What you were drinking at the time (really think about the quantities).

Give at least two or three specific examples for each topic.

SECTION I – COMPULSIVENESS

This section will help you explore just who is in control. Do you really believe it is you?

In what ways has your drinking led to the situation detailed below?

1 Accidents or dangerous situations (to myself and others).
2 Preoccupation with drink.
3 Attempts to control my drinking.
4 Loss of control of my drinking and my behaviour.

SECTION II – CHAOS

How has my inability to control my use of drink, my behaviour and my feelings affected the following?

1 My family life and social life.
2 My spiritual life (i.e. values, principles, beliefs, self-respect).
3 My work life and financial life.
4 My health.

This exercise is very similar to one I did when I was in treatment. It helped me to become honest about the consequences of my drinking and to see how I had deluded myself that I could control it. I didn't take the drink – it *took* me.

14 The little man on my shoulder

You can't hide from alcohol. It's everywhere. It's in supermarkets, off-licences, hotel rooms, most people's homes and at the beach. Alcohol can even be found in estate agents'.

I used to work at a treatment centre in Plymouth – Broadreach House. All day long I dealt with people who had drink and drug problems, listening to their awful stories and the consequences they'd suffered because of their alcohol abuse. Doing that brought up memories of my own experiences, which normally would reinforce my intentions not to pick up another drink. However, I distinctly remember leaving work one day and travelling into Plymouth to meet Josephine, my wife. We went to an estate agent's who were having a first-time buyers' evening. The first thing I was confronted with when I walked through the door was a man with a tray of wine. 'Good evening, sir. Would you like a glass of wine?' 'No thank you,' I said. 'Oh go on,' said another little voice. The man with the tray said, 'Are you sure?' I said, 'Quite sure.' 'No you're not,' said the other little voice.

The estate agent's office was full of people who were drinking wine. Now there was absolutely nothing wrong with these people drinking wine, except for what was happening to me.

The little man on my shoulder

From the moment I was confronted with the man offering me the wine, I became preoccupied with it. Even when Josephine and I sat down, the mortgage-broker had a glass of wine. I was desperately trying to concentrate on what he was saying to me, but my mind kept drifting to that glass, and I was totally preoccupied with it for the remainder of the time I sat with him.

It wasn't that I wanted to drink the wine, but I just couldn't stop hearing the voice inside my head telling me how lovely it would be – 'Just have one glass. One won't hurt you. Come on – stop being such a softie. Stop this nonsense. Why don't you just drink it? You know you want it. You've been wanting it for years, so just get on with it.' He never sleeps. He's never far away from you, and he's always listening, always waiting for a chance. He's always thirsty. One's not enough and fifty's never too many as far as he's concerned. He's the friend you don't need at any time.

'Who's he talking about?' you may well ask. I'm talking about 'the little man on my shoulder'. You've got him too. He's the one who, after you've declared that you'll never drink again, that you'll never have any more and that you're definitely on the wagon this time, says, 'Go on – stop being silly. No one will know. You're not a man if you don't drink. Stop being such a wimp.' The trouble with this little man is, if you give him any leeway, he'll plague you, he'll not let up. And, if you listen to him, he can turn a grey and dark situation into a very colourful, attractive one. He'll always tell you that things weren't that bad. He'll always tell you everything was somebody else's fault, that you weren't to blame, you're badly done by and of course you deserve a drink. 'Who wouldn't drink with all your problems?'

I call him 'the little man on my shoulder', but really he's my addiction to alcohol, and he (or my addiction) isn't going to go away. Neither is yours. You've got to be careful and vigilant, because this little man has a lot of power. If you get into the wrong frame of thinking, he can turn a perfectly comfortable situation into a nightmare in minutes.

One of the most important things to remember about your drinking is that if you become dependent on it and then you stop, the physical dependency won't be there any more, because you've stopped abusing the substance and you'll have made changes in your behaviour. However, if you pick up a drink again, that'll wake up the whole addictive process and you'll have no choice but to have another drink.

I know it sounds strange, even silly, to talk about 'the little man on my shoulder' and all the messages he gives, but, believe me, once he gets in the driving-seat you don't have much choice except to go where he takes you. Think about the last time you got really drunk, then sobered up and suddenly realized what'd been happening or how badly you felt about yourself and the way you'd behaved. That's where he takes you. He doesn't stop – you just go straight there.

I can remember very early on in my recovery, about six or seven months after I had quit drinking, I was on my way to work one morning and all of a sudden he just popped up in my thoughts and said, 'Why don't you have a drink?' I was working in a restaurant at the time, and alcohol was available. I felt really panicky, because his voice was strong and he was really convincing. I started to think, 'Well, maybe I can just have a couple.' There was one part of me convincing myself that I could have a social drink, and the other part saying, 'Don't be ridiculous. Don't be crazy. You know what you're like when you have a drink.' So on the spur of the moment I started asking myself some questions:

1 *'Well, if you were a social drinker, when would you drink?'*
My answer to that was, 'Well, I've always liked a drink in the morning, so I'd probably have a drink when I got out of bed.'

2 *'When would you drink the rest of the day?'*
My answer was, 'Of course I like to have a drink, and there's nothing wrong with it, so I'd probably carry on drinking from the time I got out of bed.'

3 *'Would it be any different at lunchtime or in the afternoon?'*
'No. I'd just carry on.'

4 *'What would you do on the way home from work?'*
'Well, I'd go for a drink – most people do. I've worked hard all day for it.'
'But you've been drinking all day.'
'Well, that's all right.'

5 *'What would you do on your day off?'*
'What do you mean? I'd be in the pub, where I'd be drinking.'

6 *'So, if you were a social drinker, Beechy, when would you drink?'*

'Well, I'd drink all the time.'

Does that sound like social drinking to you? It certainly doesn't to me. It sounds like someone who is totally out of control with his drinking and can't do anything else but drink. Silly as it sounds, this really helped me that day. It pointed out to me very quickly that, if I ever started again, I wouldn't stop. It would be the same old story, and I'd be at it all the time. It frightened me, and certainly silenced that voice inside my head.

From time to time over the years, when he's been very strong and has given me all the negative messages that sound so good, I've used that question-and-answer technique to help me again. You see, I can't make a statement like, 'I'm never going to drink again.' I'm just not going to drink for today, and, as I said before, that's much easier than making a total commitment, because it still gives me a choice.

You've got to safeguard yourself if you're planning to quit drinking, because not only does this little man sit on your shoulder, he also takes the form of other people in the most unlikely circumstances. Someone you don't know could try to get you to have a drink at a social occasion where you don't know many people. For a split second you'll feel it would be easier to drink – you'd not be the odd one out, and you'd feel less embarrassed to accept than say 'No.' Sometimes people won't take no for an answer. If someone offers me a drink, I'll make a quip like, 'I can't drink on an empty head.' If they continue, I'll say, 'I'm allergic to it.' If they keep going on at me I'll give them ten minutes on the effects that alcohol has on me and the consequences I've suffered from it, and I can assure you they'll do anything but offer me an alcoholic drink again.

Having said that, I know you don't want to go through any of this. In fact, neither do I, but sometimes it happens. So you've got to be ready, because that little man will come in different guises. He even pops up on aeroplanes – you'll hear the drinks trolley coming up behind you and everyone around is having a drink. You're sitting there and he appears and says, 'Oh go on. You're going to be on this plane for a few hours – you could always sleep it off. No one has to know. You'll be fine when you've reached your destination.' It could happen while you're on holiday – 'Doesn't everybody drink/ get drunk while they're on holiday? What's a holiday without a drink?' A holiday without a drink is probably a very thirsty one, but it doesn't have to be an alcoholic drink.

I suppose, in a way, I'm talking about a protection plan. I'm talking about ongoing support that I certainly need, and which I use effectively. I enjoy life without a drink. I enjoy my sobriety and all the things that sobriety has brought to me. I'm very protective about my well-being. If you choose to stop drinking, you'll become the same way as time goes by. You won't want back what it took so long to give up, and, silly though the 'the little man on my shoulder' scenario sounds, believe me it's very, very true.

As you're reading this, he may be talking to you – something along the lines of, 'Listen to this bullshit! This guy must be crazy. Stop reading this nonsense. Why don't you have a drink to prove him wrong? You know you can. You can quit any time you want, so don't read any more of this garbage. Throw it in the bin or put it back on the shelf.' I suppose in lots of respects I'm asking you who's in charge. Him or you? Ask yourself who's in charge right now as you're reading this page. Which messages are the strongest: the ones coming from me, or the ones coming from him (or her, as the case may be)? The main message throughout this book is about *you* getting back into the driving-seat. It's about *you* being in charge of your life, your actions, your behaviour, your well-being and your happiness. It's about *you* taking responsibility and maintaining the dignity and self-respect you deserve to have. However, the message he'll give you is that I'm trying to take away something useful, something that gives you courage and confidence and makes you a better person. You have to decide who you're going to listen to.

Through positive thinking, you can make the decision to do something about your drinking and change the rules that govern your behaviour, and it'll be a great safeguard against the negative message that he's so good at giving. Stay positive and you'll act positive. Don't think that he'll fall off your shoulder or go away, because he won't. He'll always be there, waiting for your moment of weakness.

Someone once said to me, 'If you forget where you came from, you'll go back there.' What that person meant is this: if you forget what's been happening to you and the bad experiences you've had with alcohol, then, over a period of time, drinking won't feel so bad and may even seem an attractive option. So keep an inventory in your head of what's been happening, and use it as a safeguard when the little man on your shoulder decides to have a conversation with you, and makes you a lot of offers that will be very difficult to refuse.

15 Changing the rules

Ask yourself this: are you living for yourself or for alcohol? I ask you this question because I'd like to find out who's in charge, who's running the show – you or your alcohol? Your answer will determine how easy or difficult it's going to be to change the rules that govern your drinking.

You may answer this question by saying very quickly, 'I'm in charge. The alcohol doesn't tell me what to do. I can drink when I want and not drink when I want. I'm the boss, not the booze.' OK, well let's have a look at what's been happening:

Make a list of the hobbies, pastimes, sports and activities that you used to get a lot of pleasure from but you don't do any more. Ask yourself why you're not doing them any more, and be honest about this. Alternatively, if you are still doing some of these activities and pastimes, ask yourself how *well* you're doing them. What's your performance like? Could it be better? Why isn't it?

Don't use the old excuses: 'Well, I haven't got the time,' or 'I'm not as young as I used to be and this is as good as I'm

---

going to get.' This assignment is concerned with the extent to which your alcohol abuse gets in the way of activities and hobbies, so don't veil the answers with anything else.

Now look at how alcohol has changed the rules about your values and beliefs:

List some of the things you'd never have done before but which you've ended up doing. For example:

- Was there a time when you would have said, 'I'll never drive while under the influence of alcohol'?
- Have you found yourself spending money on alcohol that wasn't meant to be spent on alcohol? Maybe the money was supposed to be spent on your children, on something for your home or on something you really needed yourself. However, the alcohol came first.
- Can you remember a time when you never used to shout at your wife/husband and children, and when you never used to have arguments with your friends?
- Can you remember never having time off work, but now you often have time off because of your drinking? These days you find yourself asking other people to make excuses and cover for you – basically to tell lies for you – giving reasons why you can't be on the job.
- Can you remember a time when you didn't have anger and resentment towards people – your wife/husband, boss, friends, colleagues, people in general?

- Can you remember when you weren't so touchy? When you were humorous, giving and always wanting to help? Now you find yourself closed off to people, more reluctant to discuss things with them. You feel more isolated.

These are just a few examples. You need to make a list of your own, and look at what's been happening. I don't care how trivial the things are that you put down: if they're important to you and they represent your values and beliefs, then put them down on paper. It's important that you get a picture of how the rules have changed since your drinking has changed.

We're three-quarters of the way through this book, and the time's coming when you're going to have to start making some decisions about what you're going to do. You've had plenty of outlines, diagrams, scenarios, stories, suggestions, tips and support, but none of them are going to be worth anything if you don't start changing the rules. You need to be in charge, not the booze.

It could be, by now, that you've taken up some suggestions in the earlier chapters and you're actually getting some benefits. I really do hope that's the case; in fact, I know you'll be benefiting if you've done that. But if you've been sitting on the fence and waiting for me to come up with some magical way out of your problem, then forget it. You're the magic. You're the solution. You've got the answers.

It's probably been said to you before that you need some

will-power. Well, will-power basically means the power to choose, and – believe it or not – you do have that power. You just need to make the decision that you're worth changing the rules for. Let me help you with a new first rule:

Stop fighting yourself

Stop fighting against the better side of you. For example, can you remember when you were drinking recently but were supposed to be somewhere else, or when you said you'd be home at a certain time but you decided to have a couple more? A voice inside you said, 'You should be home. Your wife/husband's expecting you,' or 'You have an appointment.' There was another voice saying, 'To hell with it. Have a couple more. Tell them you couldn't get any transport, the train was late or the tube was delayed. Tell them you didn't feel well.' There was a conflict, a fight. Usually the alcohol won, and that's what I meant earlier when I asked who's in charge. Who's the boss here?

You may be angry with me for asking this, and you may still maintain that you're the boss. Well, you're probably the boss when you get up in the morning, but the minute you have a drink things change, don't they? All the good intentions go out the window. The one-hour lunches become two hours, or maybe you're even drinking before lunchtime. Whatever the situation, you've got to stop fighting yourself. Remember what I talked about in the last chapter – 'the little man on your shoulder'. If you have a conflict and you're fighting with yourself, you can be sure

that he'll be in there and he'll be screaming long and hard
on the side of alcohol.

What's the point of drinking alcohol? You don't seem to be
any good at it any more – if you really think you are, what
are you doing reading this book? Was this the only one on
the shelf? Shouldn't you be reading one on the benefits of
alcohol? I wish you luck in finding that book, and if you do
it'll take you about two and a half minutes to read it. What's
the point of this endless battle? You're supposed to be happy
with your life and enjoying yourself. Make the best of it, start
today.

Rule 2 should be:

Positive thinking

Gear yourself to a positive attitude. I don't mean that you've
got to run around with a big smile on your face all day, or tell
everyone what you're doing. You can just start gently by
knowing that you're going to make a decision, and that
you're getting back into the driving-seat and *you're* going to
be in charge of what you do and don't do. Just knowing that
you're capable of doing this, and knowing that you're capable
of making a decision like this after such a long time, will
really make you feel good and worthwhile.

You can tell someone about this if you wish – it's up to you.
If I sound hesitant, it's because you've probably made a lot of
promises about your drinking before: 'I won't do it again', 'I'll

quit tomorrow', 'This is the last one', and so on. I'm slightly hesitant in case you say to someone close, 'I'm definitely going to do something this time,' and they turn around and say, 'I've heard all this before. Sure you're going to do it – I remember the last time you said that.' That kind of reaction will not help you get off to a good start, so it may be a good idea to keep the decision to yourself for the time being. Don't make a big fuss, because this is for you. Don't worry about other people for the moment – they'll get the benefits. Put yourself first in this.

If, on the other hand, you do want to tell someone, it might be a good idea to find someone who has had a problem with his or her drinking and has done something about it. You may think, 'I don't know anybody who's had a problem with alcohol.' Have a good, hard think. You may have forgotten, or you may have a friend who has a friend with a problem, or you may want to ring one of the many self-help groups there are on offer. I've given some information on those in Chapter 18. Whoever it is, try to make sure that you can trust them to keep your confidence and to give you support. You'll need support.

What I'm asking you to do is difficult, I know that. But I also know that, once you make the decision, you can keep to it and you'll very quickly reap the benefits. The first benefit will be the affirmation of actually following through a decision and sticking to it.

Another rule can be:

Get some exercise

How fit are you? Before you put the book down, I'm not going to talk about training to be a marathon runner or a long-distance walker, going to aerobics four times a week or going on a strict diet: I'm just asking you to look at your physical condition. Could you do with some more exercise? I don't mean walking to the pub and back: I mean healthy exercise. Would you like to look different? You're going to have some extra time on your hands.

Fitness doesn't necessarily mean exercise: it also has a lot to do with your eating habits. If you've been drinking a lot, one of two things may have happened. You may not be eating a lot, or you may be eating the wrong foods – foods which are high in fat, fried foods, junk food – at the wrong times, instead of eating healthily. Think about eating what's good for you rather than what it's convenient to throw together. The majority of people who drink too much aren't known for their good nutritional habits. Look at your eating pattern.

The form of exercise is up to you. In your list of former hobbies and pastimes, sport may well have been included. If it has been neglected, you may want to take it up again – not too strenuously to start with, but gently. If you've been inactive for a while and the only thing you've been lifting is your right or left hand with a glass in it, then you may find it rather difficult to start with. So gently does it.

Getting physically fit will also mean getting mentally fit. Once you start to change the rules about your eating and your fitness, you'll really start to feel good, because physically and mentally you'll start to change and you'll notice it. You'll start to feel better about yourself. You'll start to look better. Your eyes won't look like two bottles of tomato juice – they'll have a sparkle in them again. You'll be alert and bright.

The next could be:

Think about your appearance

Are you happy with your appearance, your posture and the way your hair is? When was the last time you really looked at yourself? Are you happy with the clothes you wear? 'I can't afford to change the way I look,' you may say. Well, if you're not drinking you're going to have some extra money. I'm not talking about going out to buy a complete new wardrobe: I'm just talking about having a look. You may be perfectly happy with the way your appearance is. If that's the case, great! If not, consider making some changes. Whether we like it or not, we let ourselves go while we're drinking. We may think we look OK, but the reality is somewhat different. A good way to measure this is to have a photograph taken of yourself before you stop drinking, and another about two weeks after giving up. Have a look at those photographs, and take a look in the mirror. You'll see what I mean.

The changes you're making will start from the inside and

work out, and it'll be very noticeable that something different is happening to you, because you'll be acting differently. Your mood will be different, especially if you've stopped fighting yourself. You won't be walking around feeling resentful, with a chip on your shoulder. When someone says to you, 'What's wrong?', you won't reply with, 'Oh, I've had to stop drinking, because . . .' For once in your life you can start to hold your head up, because you're actually doing something that you don't have to make excuses about, and you don't have to tell lies. You're actually doing something for you.

Changing the rules is also going to bring you a lot of happiness. Don't think that life's going to be miserable and doom and gloom, because it's not. It'll only be that way if you choose for it to be that way. If you're starting off from a positive point, then positive it'll stay. Your list of new rules can be as long as you want – there are no guidelines for when to stop.

As I'm writing this, I'm feeling really excited for you, because I know what it's like. I made my list, and at the time it felt really strange because I thought to myself, 'Gosh, if only I could do these things. If only I could follow this through instead of failing all the time.' Well, I made my mind up, and I made my decision, and I followed the list as best I could. I didn't succeed with everything, but with most things I did, and the change has been wonderful.

Anyway, don't let me hold you up. Start on your list today, and remember: you're in charge, you're the boss, not the booze.

16 Unused potential

At The PROMIS Recovery Centre, where I work, we treat people from all walks of life and from many countries throughout the world, with different cultures and backgrounds. Their addictions may differ, but the consequences that they've been experiencing in their lives, through whatever substance they've been abusing, are equally serious and devastating. They also have a large store of unused potential in common.

More often than not this potential has not been exploited, because all their energies have been going into their drinking, drug use, abuse of food, gambling or whatever their addiction may be. One of the delights for me in my job is to see that unused potential reveal itself in many different ways.

Once the fog of alcohol starts to clear, you'll be amazed at what you'll see. Have you thought about your unused potential? Talents that you have which you don't use? Think for a moment: how much time have you really given to improving the things you are good at, let alone the talents which you may have never done anything about? Probably not a lot. Ask yourself why. If you're honest, the answer you may come up with is, 'Most of my time is taken up with my drinking.' Consequently, most other things in your life have gone by the board.

You can argue by saying, 'Well, I still do my job.' But how well do you do it? How conscientious can you be while you're under the influence of alcohol? Can you really be giving 100 per cent to your job? Can you really be part of a team? If you're self-employed can you really give your profession your full commitment? Are you meeting the deadlines and expectations that this involves? Are you going in to work every day? How many breaks are you taking? How long is your lunchbreak? How much is left 'until tomorrow', and, when tomorrow comes, how much of yesterday's work gets done? On it goes.

I'm not going to budge on this one, because I know that you can't function properly while you're under the influence of alcohol. There's no way that you can think straight, make decisions, give clear directives or be able to concentrate properly and work to your full potential. You just can't do it. You know it, and I know it, so let's forget that argument and talk about your unused potential.

How does it feel when you know you can do better than you're doing now, but you just can't seem to get your act together? What's it like to watch other people overtake you and get promotion, when you know deep inside that you can do the job just as well, if not better? Yet you're overlooked. What does that feel like? How much does it hurt you? Do you just get angry and resentful? Do you make excuses and generally just feel sorry for yourself?

Is this good enough? Is this all that you're worth? Is this the way it's going to be? Frankly, yes – unless something changes, unless you really make up your mind that something's going to change and that you're going to start looking at your potential. You may say, 'I don't think I've ever had any potential', 'I've never been good at anything', 'I've never really been able to finish anything that I've started', 'I can't seem to concentrate for long periods of time.' But how hard have you really tried? Did you genuinely make up your mind that you were going to succeed at something: that you were going to finish it and make a good job of it?

How much commitment have you put into the things that you've tried in the past? Had you even made up your mind before you started something that you weren't going to make a good job of it, and that it really wasn't worth doing anyway? Well, from this moment onwards you can change all that. You can make up your mind right now that you have the potential to recover from the situation that you're in at the moment, and that you can start to channel energy into getting better. If you put a quarter of the time and energy that you use for your drinking into your recovery, just think how positive that will be. In turn, that will open up the doors of unused potential that you haven't realized you've got.

'What could this potential be?' you ask. As I've just said, you have the potential to get better if you make the choice. 'What's my academic potential like?' Well, what were you like at school? Did you get good grades in your exams? What subjects did you do best in? Were you good at languages? Were you good at English or maths? If you didn't work as

171

hard as you could've done at school, is it too late for you to do something about that? Could you go back to night school, or a college of further education? Nowdays it's not that unusual to be a mature student. Further education might be something that you'd get a lot of pleasure from, or at least quite enjoy. It would be like finishing some unfinished business. So there's one possible avenue of potential you could explore. If you were fortunate enough to go to university, then you have even more to build on.

Maybe you have the potential for the business world. Possibly you're already in the business world. If the latter is the case, then undoubtedly your performance is going to improve as you make definite changes to your alcohol dependence. If you feel you have the potential to do well in the world of business, then make some enquiries. Don't just sit and think about it, do it. Actions speak louder than words. Just look at how much *talking* there's been, as opposed to how much *doing* there's been.

Possibly you have the potential to be an entrepreneur – someone who has that wonderful knack of creating something out of nothing.

If you're a parent, you have the potential to be a 100 per cent better parent than you have been, now that you're going to do something about your drinking. That is guaranteed potential.

If you're a housewife, look at how much better a home-maker

you can become. The potential I'm talking about doesn't have to mean that it's going to be a career for you. You might be good at DIY or gardening, or maybe you're musically talented – that can give you great enjoyment and prove to be a wonderful way to relax. It can also be something that can be enjoyed by other people as well as by yourself.

Maybe you have creative talents. Can you draw? Can you paint? Do you have an eye for design? Maybe you have the potential to create things with your hands through sculpture, wordwork, architecture or designing clothes. Maybe you have the ability to write novels, short stories, children's books or poetry? Don't roll your eyes or turn your nose up – think about what you're good at. Could you even make a career out of it?

Maybe you've got the ability to organize, to be a good adminis-trator.

Maybe, like me, you have an aptitude for a helping profession. You might have great potential for helping other people to help themselves. That could take the form of becoming a doctor, a nurse, a social worker, a therapist or a counsellor. Or maybe you have the potential to work with children – that's a field where there's always a great need for skilled people. Maybe you have the ability to work with old people – it's a wonderful feeling to be able to give comfort to someone else, and if you have that potential you should most certainly use it, for it is a gift.

Maybe your potential lies in sport.

Maybe you're a chef – which is more than possible, because there are so many people in the catering profession with alcohol problems. If you are a chef, the standard of your food, your cooking of it and the way it's presented, will undoubtedly improve.

The list is endless. Isn't it exciting to think that it's possible for you to do something new with your life, or to improve on what you're already doing? Most of all, more than anything else, wouldn't it just be wonderful to be happy with yourself and not to have those feelings of shame, guilt, remorse and anxiety, and that dreaded feeling of knowing how you're going to feel the next morning because that's the way you feel every morning? That feeling of panic the minute you open your eyes as you try to get yourself together to face another day – imagine the release from that, and having the freedom to put all that behind you and not to be constantly worrying because you can't remember the night before, or that what you said may have offended or hurt someone. No more memory blackouts, no more torturing yourself, trying to justify your behaviour when you're drunk, when you know deep inside that it's ruining you and taking away everything that's good about you.

This nightmare can change, and you have the potential to change it. First and foremost, however, you must want to – when you've decided that you do, the rest will fall very quickly into place.

I've outlined many types of potential in this chapter, some of which will apply to you, some of which won't. I think it would be a good idea if *you* make a list of what you see as your potential. Be as realistic as you can. Don't set your sights too high, as it's very easy to fall into the old trap of telling yourself that it's not worth trying something because you always fail. This is a very important time for you; it's important that you stay positive.

If you're having trouble making a list of your potential, ask someone who's close to you or who knows you well. I'm sure they'll be more than willing to help you, and more than likely they'll see potential in you that you didn't realize you had. Don't procrastinate with this assignment. Do it straight away. Let's not waste any more precious time.

17 The price we pay

I remember getting very close to the first anniversary of my starting to be sober, and feeling really panicky that I wouldn't be able to make it. For me, giving up drink for ten minutes, never mind a day, a week, a month, six months or a year, was totally alien.

I'd been going to Alcoholics Anonymous meetings regularly, and one of those meetings was on a Thursday. Throughout the (nearly) twelve months that I'd been attending those meetings, several people had been celebrating their 'sober birthdays'. One of the traditions in the meeting was to have a birthday cake, because a year's sobriety is something to really celebrate. There'd been people with five, ten or fifteen candles on their cake, and I think one person in particular had twenty-one candles. The candles represented years without a drink, and I thought, 'My God! Imagine that – that's a life-time.'

I was getting close to my first year, and that meant a lot to me, because so many things had happened in that year. As I said in the Introduction, I had a job – maybe not the best-paid job in the world, but it was a job and it was something that I felt really good about. I was looking better, I had lost weight, and I had stopped shaking. Physically and mentally I was feeling so much better, and I was starting to take care of myself. And sometimes, in spite of myself, I started believing what I'd been told – that it would get better and that my life would improve if I stuck, very simply, to taking life a day at a time.

I started to get very protective about achieving a year's sobriety, and I took things to extremes – like going out of my way to cross the road in the safest place. I know this sounds silly, but it felt precious to me, and I wanted it so much. I wanted to achieve something, and I wanted to have a cake, and I wanted to get my candle on that cake.

Eventually 19 June arrived and I went to the meeting, and lo and behold there was a lovely cake with one little candle on it. I felt so proud you wouldn't believe it. There I was – 365 days without a drink. All through that meeting I remember feeling so good inside that I tried not to smile in case the other members thought that I wasn't taking things seriously!

After the meeting we had some tea – I cut the cake into slices and handed them around. There was a visitor at the meeting, and she said, 'Is your name Beechy?' 'Yes.' I replied. 'We've got a mutual friend,' she said – 'Davey.' 'Gosh!' I said. 'I haven't seen or heard of him in years.' She looked at me and said, 'Well, he's dead.'

All of a sudden her voice sounded fifty miles away, and I seemed to go deaf. I couldn't hear. 'He's dead' was stuck in my head, and I had to shake myself to snap out of it. She went on to tell me that alcohol had been the cause of his death. He had been sober for quite a while, and had said at some of his AA meetings that he had a friend whom he hadn't seen in a long time. He had said that he was desperately worried about his friend because of his drinking, and he wished that he could get him to quit and maybe help him to get sober. I felt so sad when she told me this, because the friend he had been talking about was me.

It was a short, sharp shock that brought me straight back to reality. Here I was, with my year's sobriety, feeling so good and on top of the world, and then I heard about my friend dying because of his alcoholism. It was like I was being given a message – 'Yes, you've got your year. Yes, you're doing well. But don't think that you can go back to drinking again, because it'll kill you if you do.'

I'll never forget that day and the way that I felt when I learned about my friend. I've carried the memory through my sobriety, and it's become a very positive force for me, because I know that if ever I pick up a drink again it will kill me. I can't drink any more. I'm no good at it. It doesn't work for me. I've accepted that. I know the price that ultimately has to be paid for continued abuse of alcohol: there is no way that people can survive without physical consequences, mental consequences, emotional consequences, destruction of families and relationships while they're abusing alcohol. The abuse of alcohol will reach out to everyone connected with the person abusing it and they'll all get ensnared by its destructive net.

Alcoholism is a fatal disease if it's not arrested. I use the word 'arrested' because there is no cure. A lot of people seem to think that, if they don't drink alcohol for a period of time, they will then be able to continue drinking again. That is not the case. When a person with a drinking problem puts down the drink, the consequences surrounding the drinking problem cease. If that person picks up a drink again, then he or she has got the problem back. It doesn't go away. There have been countless people who have lost their lives because of this way of thinking – they haven't had a drink for a while and they think, 'A couple won't hurt. I can go back and it won't be as bad as it was.' But once they start again they can't stop, and eventually they pay the price.

Remember my image of someone repeatedly sticking their hand into a bucket of burning petrol and screaming? You'd think that anyone who did that was crazy, wouldn't you? You would tell them to stop doing it, wouldn't you? Isn't it amazing that people suffer continued physical pain every time they have a drink, and yet they continue doing it despite advice from their doctor/consultant/family or threats from employers. Nothing changes: they just keep on doing it. Why? Quite simply, because they are *dependent* on the alcohol, and, once the dependency is there, nothing will change unless it is arrested. If not, the price, as I've said, is horrendous. Not only is death the ultimate price, but generally people will suffer from problems with the liver, the kidneys, the heart, the nervous system, the skin, the stomach and the rest of the digestive system. Frankly, if alcohol is being abused it will attack the complete physical well-being of the person.

But it doesn't stop there. Think about the accidents caused through drunken driving. Innocent people are being killed. The accident rate in the workplace due to alcohol consumption – through people who drink and then work with machinery in factories or on building sites – is very high. I wonder how many fires are started through alcohol abuse – people smoking cigarettes and falling asleep, setting fire to furniture and themselves. These are dreadful consequences which occur daily, and countless people are suffering because of them – not only the people who are abusing the alcohol, but other people who are being directly affected by this behaviour.

It is so sad to see the devastating effects on the family when someone dies through alcohol abuse. Quite recently I met the wife of a man who had died of alcoholism. She sat in my office, looked directly at me and said, 'What's left for me? I feel so empty now that he's gone.' Even though they had been living apart for quite a considerable period of time, she had hoped that her husband would eventually get well and stop drinking. But it wasn't to be. Despite all that had happened to him, such as losing his job and the respect of his colleagues, the separation from his wife, the isolation from his grown-up children, the continued effects on his health, none of it had made any difference. As far as he was concerned, he was in control of his drinking and he could quit any time he wanted to. He couldn't see what was happening to him, and because of the denial of his dependence on alcohol he couldn't hear what was being said to him. Inevitably he died from his drinking. The effects still linger on, because his wife is left with memories of someone who didn't always drink, of someone who was an immensely kind and generous man, and who at one time had been a very good father and husband. He had also been extremely good at his job and had been very responsible until the alcohol took over. Bit by bit, his life got out of control, and he lost everything – including his life. Now his wife sits with just the thoughts of what might have been. It is such a waste of a life. It is so unnecessary, but it happens – and it will continue to happen.

In the next fifteen to twenty minutes, and every fifteen to twenty minutes, there will be two drink-driving convictions and two emergency medical admissions, one admission to psychiatric hospital and one death from alcohol abuse. It's not going to get any better. I know that, if you make a decision, you need not be one of these statistics. You need not suffer these serious consequences. The choice is yours. The responsibility is yours. All you need to do is make a decision that you want things to change, that you are willing to do some work, that you are willing to ask for some help, that you're going to be honest with yourself and others. Otherwise, understand that the price you are paying physically, mentally and emotionally will at the end of the day totally bankrupt you. Ask yourself: is this the price you want to pay? Does your drinking mean so much to you that you're willing to sacrifice everything – your wife or husband, your children, your family, people who love you and care for you?

Before you answer that question, look back over the assign-ments you have done in this book. Look at the consequences, look at the effects that your alcohol has had on your life. This should help you come to the healthy decision you need to make. If you haven't experienced many of these consequences, and you don't feel that your drinking at this moment is so bad, then I ask you to think again. Count yourself lucky that you haven't had to go through this hell and torment. This is an equally important time for you to make a decision – if you continue, you *will* have these consequences. No one who continually abuses alcohol escapes the price that must be paid.

18 You're not alone

I used to think that I was the only person who drank like I did, behaved like I did and even *felt* like I did. For years, even though people told me, pointed me in all sorts of directions and tried to help me, I never really believed that there was anybody else who actually felt the same as me.

It may sound as if I'm making myself out to be very special and different, even being grandiose to suggest that nobody felt the same loneliness, despair, isolation, remorse, anger and guilt that I felt. I think it would be more truthful to say that I just didn't notice other people, because I was so self-obsessed and self-centred. I was interested only in me.

During all those years when people tried to point me in the right direction, I didn't listen. I didn't take any notice, and I was probably quite rude to them, mainly because I only wanted to be pointed in the direction of another drink, certainly not to go in a direction which would take me away from it.

If you've had feelings that people are trying to take something away from you, well, they are. However, you see it as them trying to take away from you something that you love and which is a great comfort to you; but, as you and I have been discussing in this book, alcohol is really *not* a comfort. It certainly doesn't love you, and it's been taking you down all the wrong roads. It's brought you to here.

Another reason why I used to think that nobody felt or drank like I did was because I would never *talk* about my feelings. I would certainly never talk about my drinking. Why would I if I was convinced that I wasn't drinking too much? So, just like you, I've had those feelings, and at certain times in my life while drinking I've felt total despair because I believed that no one would understand if I told them how I felt.

Have you ever watched a couple of drunken people in a pub having a conversation? Isn't it interesting how, when you're under the influence of alcohol, you suddenly become bilingual? You can suddenly speak another language. Think back to those drunks in the pub: one of them's talking rubbish, but the other one will be nodding, understanding. It's quite funny to watch, but also very boring to be on the receiving end – especially if you're sober.

Let's get honest: how many times have you honestly and openly *talked* to someone about your drinking when you haven't had a drink? Think about it. I'd imagine not very often, if at all. Most people who drink too much will discuss it when they're feeling remorseful or very down, and that's usually when they're under the influence of alcohol: their tongues loosen, and maybe for once they're not being abusive or defensive. They'll open their hearts to someone and tell them how they're feeling, even though the following day they'll not remember anything about it. If the conversation is repeated to them, they'll probably deny it and say, 'Oh, I was just being silly. I was just joking. Don't believe any of that.'

Isn't it sad that you have to deny your feelings? Isn't it even sadder that the only way you can talk about your feelings is usually under the influence of alcohol? I can understand this. It's so frightening to let someone in, mainly because you may actually have to follow through from what you've been saying and start to do something about your drinking.

Let's suppose for a moment that you are going to follow this through, and that you are going to do something. The first question usually is, 'Where can I go for help?'

Most people go to see their doctors, because doctors are supposed to know everything and to have the answers to most problems. Doctors are usually seen as 'safe' people to talk to, who have your best interests at heart. With most doctors, I believe this to be the case. Go along to your doctor and ask for his or her advice, and hopefully he or she will have good information regarding drink problems. I use the words 'good information', because I believe that there's also bad information available, and it's my intention to give you the best help that I can and the best advice to help you with your problem.

This is only my personal opinion, but let's look at what I see as a piece of bad information: 'Control your drinking.'

Well, the simple reply to that is that if you could control your drinking you wouldn't be asking for help. You've already tried to control your drinking. You've been trying for a long, long time, and it just hasn't worked. How do you control what's out of control? We're not talking about social drinking any more, and we're not talking about the sort of drinking that everyone else is doing: we're talking about you very possibly being dependent on alcohol. Dependency doesn't cease with the continual use of it.

In my personal and professional opinion, the only way to deal with dependency on alcohol is *abstinence*. Let's face it, you're no good at drinking any more. If you were, then you and I wouldn't be having this conversation. Abstinence is the key to your freedom. Controlling your drinking is not. In my opinion, recommending controlled drinking is like saying to a compulsive wife-beater, 'Beat her only three times a week instead of five.' It's ludicrous and totally unprofessional for someone to say to you, 'Try to control it,' when it's causing you and people around you so many problems. Stop drinking alcohol, and the problems surrounding your alcohol abuse will cease. You'll still have your feelings to contend with, and all those underlying fears that you've been trying to quell with alcohol will still be there, but at least you can start to make a move in the right direction: to talk about those feelings and to understand them, to come to terms with the issues that've really been bothering you. There's no way to solve an alcohol problem while you're still drinking.

The most successful self-help group I know that exists in the world today is the first number in your telephone book: Alcoholics Anonymous. AA does nothing but work, if you choose to follow the very simple programme that it offers. There are AA meetings *everywhere*. Wherever you live, there's an AA meeting not too far away. All you've got to do is pick up the telephone and you'll very quickly learn that you're not alone. There are countless people who feel like you do and who've found a bridge to normal living through the Twelve Steps of AA.

One of the most important things about the AA programme is that it's *anonymous*. You can feel safe at the meetings. You can share your experiences, strength and hope in the knowledge that they'll stay in that room. What a sense of freedom not to have to wear around your neck labels like 'I'm an alcoholic', 'I have a drinking problem', 'I can't stop drinking.' You don't have to do that any more. You can quite simply get on with your life, while at the same time getting an enormous amount of support from people who understand how you feel.

Having said that, you may be one of those people who cannot stop drinking simply by going to meetings of AA. You may need to be detoxified from alcohol, and this would more than likely be done in a residential setting:

- There are hospitals that offer a detoxification service.
- There are psychiatric hospitals that incorporate a detoxification unit.
- There are treatment centres.

There's a marked difference between the three. The first difference is that when you're detoxified in a hospital you're simply taken off whatever it is you've been abusing. In simple terms, you're left with yourself. But without some education, knowledge and understanding of what's been happening to you, you won't have any foundation on which to build your abstinence. It's very easy to stop drinking – staying stopped is the difficulty. Without continued help and support you'll find it very hard, if not impossible, to stay away from alcohol.

The support needs to come from a lot of quarters: family, friends, employers. People around you need to understand what's been happening to you to be able to help you, but first and foremost *you* have to be given that information. Possibly the people around you can then be incorporated into that process.

If you're looking for residential help, detoxification alone may not be sufficient. You may need something else. In the psychiatric setting you could be offered group therapy and counselling, which can be of immense help. In a treatment centre offering the Minnesota Model form of treatment, you would be given the opportunity to look at your emotional, physical, mental and spiritual well-being. This sort of treatment takes place through lectures, group therapy, one-to-one counselling, relaxation and spirituality groups. Above all, it helps you work through the first Five Steps of the AA programme. These Steps are very simple but extremely effective in helping you *arrest* the behaviour (and I emphasize the word 'arrest' – there's no cure for the underlying condition).

In the treatment centre where I work, we've taken it quite a few steps further, because we believe in cross-addictions. I myself have not met an addicted person with only one addiction. Usually people stop abusing one thing and start abusing another, whether it's food, drugs, compulsive spending, over-exercising or gambling. Addiction doesn't come with only one focus: it can very quickly switch to something else.

The treatment I'm involved in incorporates psychodrama, role-play, and experiential therapy through such things as collages, art therapy and guided imagery. We look at the patients' needs rather than their wants, and we also treat the addict as a person rather than just an addict. What I mean by that is instead of saying, 'Here comes a drinking problem', '. . . a food problem', '. . . a drug problem', '. . . an exercise problem,' we say, 'Here comes a human being with specific and sensitive needs.' We try to look at those needs and to devise a suitable treatment plan for that person and his or her family.

Attitudes in treatment are also very important. There's got to be a measure of happiness and humour, as people don't get well on doom and gloom. Where I work, we believe in humour: if you're not going to enjoy getting better, then what's the point? I'm talking about attaining some happiness in your life instead of misery. My philosophy is very much geared to looking to the day, rather than looking at yesterday. What can you do about last week's dinner? Not a lot – but you can do something about today. You can make plans for tomorrow – get excited and motivated about the possible changes in your life, rather than constantly dwelling on the failures and turmoil of your past. I'm talking about making choices and taking responsibility, and being able to cope rather than trying to escape all the time. About positive self-esteem; self-discovery; dealing openly with people and honestly with your feelings; picking up the pieces.

If residential treatment doesn't suit you, you may want to try outpatient counselling. There are a lot of facilities offering this form of treatment. There are also a lot of counsellors/therapists who offer both one-to-one counselling and groups (either men's groups or women's groups). There's a lot of help available. All you have to do is pick up your telephone, go to your doctor or look in your local newspaper. You'll always find someone offering some form of help.

I keep a very open mind on the various treatments, as it would be unfair of me to say that only one way works. I think it's true to say that different approaches suit different people. However, I've never met a person with a drinking problem who's been able to control his or her drinking to a normal social level through the non-abstinence method – i.e. through continued drinking.

I could go on and on about the different forms of help that are available, but I've outlined the major sources, and you can find out more if you so decide. The main thing I want you to hear in this chapter is that you're not alone. At this very moment, as you're reading this book, there are countless people who feel the same. So the support is there. The help is available. You're *not* alone.

19 Will next Christmas be different?

I suppose the first question I should ask you here is, 'What was last Christmas like?'

Was it the sort of Christmas that you intended it to be? You need to think a little bit about that, because I don't know what your interpretation of Christmas is. For some people it's a time of getting together with their family and exchanging of presents – especially if they have children, because Christmas is so children-orientated. For some people it's a time of thanksgiving, a celebration. And for some people it's a time to drink more, to eat more, to make promises they can't keep – it's a time to let their hair down. It seems as though people give themselves permission at Christmas to do things they wouldn't normally do. So I have to ask you to think about what Christmas means to you.

There are even some people who don't celebrate Christmas but just carry on as normal. Did you carry on as normal? Was last Christmas any different from your other Christmases? Can you remember it? Is it hazy or blurred? Ask yourself how you behaved. Did you drink as much as you usually do? Did you drink less? Were any familiar comments made to you? You know the ones:

'Oh please don't have too much to drink when we go out.'

'Please leave the keys of the car at home.'

'Do we have to stay out so late? What about the children? What about the presents? Please don't make me go home on my own again, I'd like us to go home together. After all, it's Christmas – it's a time for family. You promised it wouldn't be like this. I thought at least you could do this for the children, if not for me.'

'You didn't spend all the money on drink, did you?'

'Where have you been? You said you were going to be at home.'

'Please don't let this Christmas be like last Christmas.'

You keep making promises, but you can never keep them.

Isn't it strange: you always seem to set out with the best of intentions about what you're going to do and what you're not going to do, yet the moment you have that first drink everything goes out the window? The promises, commitments and resolutions are soon forgotten, and what comes in their place is: 'Oh well, everything can wait. It's not that bad. I'll do it tomorrow. They won't notice. I deserve this. I don't care what they think.'

This is the attitude which arrives after a few drinks, and once it's there it's very very difficult to get rid of. Have you noticed that drunken presents don't really heal the hurt that's caused through this sort of continued behaviour? I say 'continued' because, if you're really honest with yourself, Christmas doesn't really make any difference to you, does it? Your drinking doesn't really change that much, except maybe you're drinking more.

Haven't you noticed that promises seem to be broken most of the time when you drink? The commitments are pushed aside, and comments like those I listed above about Christmas are being said to you pretty much throughout the year. I don't think I'm talking about something that's news to you, I'm talking about comments that you hear for a great deal of the time. I know you're tired of hearing them, but you're going to continue hearing them until you start to change. If you don't change, the people from whom you're getting all these messages may not stick around. They may give up.

I used to say when I was drinking that every day was Christmas: every day was somebody's birthday, engagement, christening. 'Any excuse' – that's what I'm saying. Can you identify with that? Any excuse for a drink.

As you've been reading this book, you've made lists of excuses. We've looked at the preoccupation with alcohol and at all sorts of behaviour. We're approaching the time when you really have to think, 'Are things going to be different?' Do you want things to be different? Will next Christmas be different?

It all depends on what you want and need things to be. You and I have had quite a journey through this book, and I understand how painful it's been. You've stuck with me: I know some of the time you haven't wanted to, but you have. As I say, we're coming to a time when you really need to make some decisions. Decisions about *you*. Decisions about your happiness, your self-worth, self-respect and self-esteem. Decisions about that bigger person who's inside of you and is trapped trying to get out: that good person. That person who wants people around you to know that you're not a bad person, that you do have feelings, that you're sensitive, that you're a good father/mother, that you're a good lover, that you're a good provider. That there's something more to you than just having a drink.

Next Christmas can be different. It could be so different that you'd never believe it. It could be the best Christmas present you could ever give to the people who know you. We all know that young children wait for Father Christmas to come to their home. I wonder how many children are waiting for their father or mother to come home too. In their hearts it'd be worth more to them than all the silver paper, fancy wrapping and toys that they could ever have: to see a daddy and mummy be happy. Then they'd be happy, because don't forget – I said it earlier on, in Chapter 10 (maybe you need to go back and read it) – your behaviour infects your family's behaviour. Even if you're not a parent, you're important to someone. Someone is depending on you, someone needs you. But most of all you need yourself.

This happiness I'm talking about can very easily be attained. Maybe you don't know what the word means. Maybe it's been a long time since you've experienced happiness. Maybe the only happiness that you think you can have comes from having a drink. I can assure you that there's happiness beyond your wildest dreams without alcohol and all the misery that it's bringing you. It can quite simply be attained by you making a decision *to stop drinking*.

You can argue with me all day long that you can control your drinking, that you can cut it down at any time you want, that you can quit any time you want. If that's the case, why are you reading this? If you can do all these things, why haven't you done them? I'm throwing down the gauntlet: it's time to make the decision, not to keep boasting.

If you're continually saying, 'Well, I don't have a problem with alcohol,' then it won't be a problem if you don't drink it – will it? It really won't be a problem if the last drink that you had was your last. Walking past a pub or an off-licence won't be a problem. If in fact you do go into a pub, it won't be a problem just having a soft drink. Will it? But if you can't do these things, then it is a problem and we've got to look at it. I've already talked about most aspects of this problem earlier in the book, so now you have to start making some decisions.

What do you think you need to do about all this? Don't make a decision right away – you need to think about it. Maybe you need to write down a list of your options, be honest and ask yourself, 'Can I continue this way?' If not, I've got some suggestions for you – very positive, simple suggestions.

As I've said already: you're not alone. There are thousands of people with this problem. There's help and support. It's all waiting for you, and it's just one step away. That's the step you've been getting ready to take. Remember, there's no shame in your doing this. You're not any less of a person because you're going to help yourself. You're doing something extremely *positive* for yourself. You're actually saying to yourself, 'I'm worth more than this. I deserve this. This should've happened a long time ago,' and you just have to make that decision on a daily basis.

I'm not asking you to say, 'I'll never drink again. I'll never touch another drop. I hate alcohol.' I'm not asking you to say any of those things. I'm quite simply saying to you that for one day, for twenty-four hours, you do not have to have a drink. If you want to make it less than that, you can say to yourself, 'For five minutes I don't have to do this.' It's your decision. The self-affirmation and self-esteem, the confidence that you'll begin to feel in yourself because you've made this decision, because you want to do something about your drinking, will be *enormous*. It'll help to drive you on. There's a lot more that you need to do, but this first step, this commitment, is important.

Every time you walk into a pub, an off-licence, a supermarket or wherever it is that you buy your alcohol, it's as if you're walking into a boxing-ring. You're getting beaten and knocked down, and yet you get up. You're being counted out, but you keep going back for more. It's time to throw in the towel. You know it, I know it, and that person inside you who's screaming to get out and get on with his or her life knows it. What are you waiting for? Why are you procrastinating? Is it fear of what's going to happen?

I know how frightened you feel, but I think there's more to fear about you taking your next drink than about not taking it, because if you don't have that drink then at least you know that all the things that happen when you do drink won't happen. If you do pick up that first drink, you know you're powerless and unmanageable. You know the things you do when you're under the influence. I know you don't want to do them, but you do do them, because you quite simply have no choice when you have that first drink.

So the simple decision that I'm asking you to make is to not pick it up. If you've got a glass in front of you at this very minute and you can't keep your hand from picking it up, or if you can't walk past a pub or off-licence, then there's no excuse left for you not to identify your powerlessness and unmanageability with respect to alcohol.

I'm very excited about what this decision that you're contemplating can actually mean for you, because I made my decision, and the resulting excitement and change in my life doesn't seem to stop – it just keeps going on and on for the better. Life has its ups and downs, but not as many as when I was drinking. Someone once said to me, 'Your worst day in recovery is nothing like as bad as when you were drinking.' It's true: things can only get better if you decide to make some changes.

Maybe a good idea would be to think about the last four or five Christmases. What were they like? Did you enjoy yourself? Did everybody around you have a good time? If you have difficulty remembering, then ask your wife/husband/ girlfriend/boyfriend or your children. Your children will remember very clearly, because, as I said, Christmas is an important time to them. Think about the way you used to look forward to Christmas when you were little and how important it was to you that you had a happy time.

I've given you a lot to think about in this chapter, so I'll leave it here. The decision's yours.

20 Where do we go from here?

Before we go any further, let's have a recap and take stock of where we are at the moment. We've covered a lot of ground in the last nineteen chapters, and I think it's extremely important for you to relate this to yourself and build up a picture of your drinking pattern.

Right at the outset of the book, you were given the chance to define what constitutes a drinking problem and to decide through a very basic questionnaire whether you have a drinking problem. It's more than possible that you accepted that you had a drinking problem before you even looked at that chapter – even before you bought the book. Either way, it's been an important exercise for you to define clearly what you see as a problem, because you're the one who's drinking. You're the one who has all the answers.

We've talked about alcoholics not coming in bottles – they come in people. You are a person, an individual. Unless you've an identical twin, there's no one exactly like you – who laughs like you, with your sense of humour, who thinks exactly the same as you. That makes you an individual person with individual needs. It's important, while you're reading this book, that you think about you, and that you consider you, because the changes you're looking at making, and the decisions you're contemplating, are for you.

We've talked about the cravings for alcohol. We've looked at the issue that it's not the amount you're drinking, it's the wanting to drink that's the problem – the need for alcohol, the comfort of it, the stability you think it gives you.

We've looked at the possibility of your cutting down your drinking with a view to quitting and trying abstinence, rather than continually trying to control your drinking (which doesn't seem to work at all for you).

We've looked extensively at the behaviour of a person with a drinking problem. I know that wasn't easy to read about, but neither is it easy to live with, nor is it easy to watch someone inflict such behaviour on themselves. I once read that alcoholism is a disease which tells you that you haven't got a disease. How true! Think about the way you deny your drinking; the way you've gone to any lengths to shrug off your behaviour, to pass the responsibility for your behaviour on to someone else. You've used any defence to maintain your habit, because that's what it's become – a habit: a way of life, a behaviour which has encompassed you as a person and which dictates in most if not all areas of your life precisely what you do.

We've looked at other people's stories – at people who've been abusing alcohol and what's happened to them. Hopefully you have identified with their feelings, and possibly with some of the circumstances they've experienced because of their drinking.

We've talked about you falling into the trap of thinking that you're a bad person, when you're not. Your natural behaviour is very different from your drinking behaviour – your real personality is very different from what alcohol has made you become. It's like Dr Jekyll and Mr Hyde – you're perfectly normal to begin with, but after a few drinks things start to change, and after some more drinks the mood-swings really take effect and you become someone else. But it's the alcohol provoking the negative change in you, so it's important for you to separate yourself from it. Don't denounce yourself as a bad person.

We've talked about your alcohol in terms of a relationship – a love affair – and about the preoccupation you have with it: about how you even hide your alcohol to protect your supply. Probably without your even realizing it, alcohol has become the love of your life and has started to take precedence over everything else. You can deny this, but I'm asking you to look at the way you behave. If alcohol is a big part of your life, then there are other parts of your life that are being affected because of your drinking. It's a simple fact, but it's very difficult to accept.

We've had a look around your 'house inside', and at how you suppress your feelings and use alcohol to block out a lot of them.

We've looked at how you put defences in front of your feelings so you don't have to talk about them, and how painful that is and what a web of deception it weaves.

Empty bottles and broken promises – look at the power that alcohol has had in your life. Look at the dominant role it plays. Your drinking isn't really social any more, is it?

The family, the forgotten partners, the children who grow up so quickly and the moments which are lost and can never again be recaptured. The way they suffer. Oh! so painful, but so important to look at, think about and understand. You've got to get the whole picture of what's been happening to you, and realize that there are other people involved – you're not the only one with the hardship and emotional pain.

Making choices? You've got loads of them. There are so many choices you can make in a positive direction. They're all just waiting for you.

Remember those magical myths of alcohol:

- 'I can't laugh without a drink'?
- 'Life would be dull without a drink'?
- 'I won't know how to spend my time'?
- 'Only tramps are alcoholics'?
- 'All alcoholics drink in the mornings'?
- 'People will find me boring if I don't drink'?

and so on.

Where do we go from here?

In Chapter 13 we talked about 'keep doing what you're doing and you'll keep getting what you've got.' We went through the early stage, the middle stage, the crucial stage and the chronic stage of drinking. Remember the self-assessment that you completed in that chapter, where I asked you to give specific examples about your drinking?

Don't forget the little man on your shoulder – the little man who doesn't go away – the little man who's always ready to pounce when you're feeling vulnerable, tired or miserable. He'll always be there to encourage you to solve your problems by having a drink, so let's not forget him.

We looked at how alcohol has changed the rules about your values and beliefs, and how you could set this straight by making a list of your own rules, to do things differently. Think about all the unused potential which is waiting to be unleashed, and just how much you can achieve if you really put your mind to it.

The price we have to pay should never be forgotten. If you keep doing what you are doing you'll pay a high price, but if you decide to do something about your drinking then the price is relatively small for the enormous benefits you're going to get.

There's comfort in knowing that you're not alone. You're not the only one suffering because of alcohol – there are countless other people who feel exactly the same as you do but who have made a decision and are doing something very positive about their lives. It's important for you to draw strength from the knowledge that there is hope and help, and that there is happiness for you.

Will next Christmas be different? It most definitely will if you're going to make a decision to follow the guidelines in this book. It'll be the best Christmas you've ever had.

So that's where we've got to so far. Give yourself a big pat on the back – you've done an enormous amount of work. You've absorbed a great deal of information, and I've asked you many questions to which I hope you've found some answers.

In Chapter 4 I asked you to make a plan for the day, and now it's time to re-evaluate that plan. If you decided to cut down your drinking, how did it go? Were you able to stick to the amount you decided upon, or did you have one or more drinks over that amount? Was it hard for you to put down the glass, or put the top on the bottle, or walk out of the pub, or not go to the off-licence, or refuse the drink? How did it feel? It's very important to think about this, because it gives you a clear picture of just how much in or out of control you are with your drinking.

If you decided to take the big step and stopped drinking, how's it been? Was it more or less difficult than you thought? Have you been able to sustain your abstinence every day, or have you had the occasional drink? What's the reaction been like from people around you – family, friends, people you work with, people you socialize with? Have you had a lot of support from them?

However it's been, congratulate yourself for tackling the assignment. It takes a lot of courage to face up to what we've been talking about so far in this book.

Perhaps it's time to take the plan a step further. I hope that by now you'll have begun the self-assessment assignment in Chapter 13. Remember that? Have you been looking at the effects of alcohol on most areas of your life? Refer back to it, and take a good look at what's been happening – before we can go anywhere else, you have to look at the picture, or as much as we've painted so far. What do you think? Do you want to continue doing what you're doing – are you happy with the way things are? Do you really feel in control of your behaviour with alcohol?

You have to ask yourself where *you* want to go from here, because I'm writing this book from a bias – I've quit drinking. I made my decision, and I'm seeing the benefits from that. The changes that have happened to me have been very positive, but, as I've said, I had to take the appropriate steps and work extremely hard to maintain my sobriety. I had to make my decision for myself, and I had to take the first step.

Your next step is totally up to you. The very fact that you've got this far in the book clearly tells me that you want to do something about your drinking. I've already said that I can't teach you to drink socially, or to drink like 'a lady' or 'a gentleman', but I've given you the choice to decide what you want to do. I've given you the option of *trying* to control your drinking. I've emphasized the word 'trying' because I don't believe you *can* control your drinking and be happy with it. For argument's sake, let's assume that you've tried to cut down, but you haven't been successful and you've ended up drinking the same (if not more), and your behaviour isn't getting any better. The consequences aren't getting any easier, and the pressure you're under from other people is increasing. That can only mean that you're becoming more and more isolated and withdrawn within yourself, and you're beginning to feel more trapped inside the bottle. So you really do need to go somewhere from here. You can't stay in this place, because this is serious – it's going to get worse, and it's going to get worse very quickly, so you have to make some positive decisions. Time is running out. You've been lucky to get this far with your drinking, and your luck isn't going to last for ever.

The first decision you can make is to use the information I've given you so far in this book. That will quickly set you on the right course to arrest your drinking problem.

The second decision you can make is to take responsibility and set yourself some short-term realistic goals. For example:

1 You're not going to expect too much too quickly.
2 You're going to ask for help, accept it, and realize that it's not what you want that's important: it's what you need that's going to be good for you. At this present moment you don't know what you need, and that's why you're going to have to trust the advice you're being given.
3 Stick with the people who are supportive to you. You'll find these people in the self-help groups I've mentioned.

4 Accept that you haven't been the most wonderful person in the world, or the easiest person to live with, so it's going to take a while to regain the trust of the people who are close to you.

Don't despair if you don't get it right. You're a human being – you're allowed to make mistakes. Don't lose your sense of humour. You're not making all these changes to be miserable – we're talking about you being happy; we're talking about you having some rewards in your life and about enjoying yourself and having some fun. Break free from the trap you've been in.

The third decision you can make is to really go somewhere from here, rather than back to where you've been.

21 Letting go

Searching for the strength within us:
    Have we got it? I don't know.
Is it fear that holds us back from
    Letting go?

Do we really have to face this?
    How much do they need to know?
Isn't there some other way of
    Letting go?

What's this feeling called surrender?
    Am I putting on a show?
I'm so fearful of rejection
    If I let go.

My real self is just a memory,
    I've become a hell to know.
Will I wake up from this nightmare
    If I let go?

Searching for the strength within us:
    Have we got it? I don't know.
Is it fear that holds us back from
    Letting go?

Letting go

These are the lyrics to a song I wrote about two years ago, and for me they depict my fear when someone said to me, 'You've got to let go.'

Let go of what? Let go of the past, let go of the old behaviour, let go of the memories, let go of the self-doubts, criticisms, insecurities and fears. As the first line of the first verse suggests, I had to search for the strength within me to do this. At that time I really didn't know what I was going to do, because 'Let go' seemed like such an odd suggestion. It may be easier to picture something in your hand and someone saying, 'Put it down and don't pick it up again.' Look at it that way if you like.

I'm saying that it's time to put down the glass, to put down the bottle, and to stop picking up what seems to keep giving you a lot of heartache and not much enjoyment. It seems so straightforward when you think of it like this, doesn't it? 'Why do you keep doing this? Why don't you just let go? Stop doing it!' But it's not that easy, is it? You've tried in the past, and you've always picked the glass up again, but that doesn't mean you're a failure – it doesn't mean that you can't do it or that you're a hopeless case. I believe it's because you weren't ready.

Once something has got a hold on you emotionally, physically and mentally, it's not easy to say, 'That's it – I'm not doing it again,' because there are so many things involved. There are a lot of external pressures you have to cope with. I'm saying that stopping drinking is more than putting down the drink:

it's staying stopped that's the problem. To succeed in this, you've got to let go of more than just the alcohol.

As the lyrics of the song say, 'Do we really have to face this? How much do they need to know?' It's not only a question of how much *they* need to know, it's how much do *you* have to face up to *yourself*. Undoubtedly, the more you look the more you'll see and the more you'll find out, and so the more you'll be able to change. Someone said to me recently, 'You've got to say hello before you can say goodbye.' You've got to take a look at yourself and face up to what it is you want to change – what you don't particularly like about yourself – before you can change it.

I'm not talking about tearing yourself to bits and doing a total character assassination: I'm asking you to be realistic about what your behaviour is like when you're drinking, and how much that suits the way you really are and want to be. If you're honest and realistic, you'll very quickly see that the behaviour you like doesn't match the behaviour you display while you're under the influence of alcohol. It's not that you're a bad person: it's just that when you drink alcohol it changes your behaviour. I think it's time to ask yourself what you're holding on to, and why it's so important that you should continually feel like this. Why do you keep punishing yourself? Is it because you don't care? Is it because you don't think you're worth changing for? Is it because you think it's too late to change?

Maybe you don't want to change – you want to continue

with everything that drinking means. I really doubt that, because you wouldn't have got so far in this book if you didn't really care, and if you didn't really want to change, and if you didn't really think you're worth it. All you've got to do is make a decision that you're going to let go and begin the process of salvaging yourself, and regain your self-respect for *you* – not for anyone else.

As I've said all the way through this book, it's important that this is for you. Believe me, once you start to let go of the old behaviour, you'll wonder why you held on to it for so long and were so protective of it, when really what you were protecting was something that was making most of your life miserable. Think about it. Aren't you worth more than that? Isn't it time things got better for you? Well, here's your opportunity. Here's your chance for changes to take place. Letting go of what you don't want means making room for things that you need, like regaining people's trust; getting self-respect; recovering your dignity; finishing things that you start rather than giving up halfway through; being comfortable with yourself rather than putting on an act most of the time; being able to look people straight in the eye without feeling that they're going to find out something about you, or ask you about something you did that you can't remember doing because you were drunk.

It'll be such a relief to have all those embarrassing situations stop. In fact, to begin with it'll feel very strange because all of a sudden you won't have to be running around with a load of alibis and excuses – your behaviour will have changed, so you won't need them. However, don't expect everyone to change with you. A lot of your drinking partners won't really understand why you're doing this and they may not be very encouraging about your change of behaviour. If anything, they'll probably go out of their way to encourage you to stay as you were. This may become a real conflict for you, because if you're deciding to let go of a certain way of life you can't keep two sets of books. For example, it'll be hell on earth if you try to continue going to the pub or club, or wherever it is that you meet up with your drinking partners, when suddenly you're not drinking. You'll be among people who are doing what (to start with) you still want to do. Though you're trying to break away from it, because deep inside you know that it doesn't work for you any more, you can't expect them to encourage you *not* to drink when they're still drinking, so you'll receive comments such as:

'*Oh, just have one.*'

Or:

'*Just have a half instead of a pint.*'

Or:

'*One won't hurt you.*'

Or:

'*Just have a couple. A couple of drinks never hurt anyone. Stop being stupid. Stop being silly. Stop being such a sissy. What's happened to you all of a sudden? You're no fun any more. You're boring. Have you become religious? You know you always play darts better with a couple of pints inside you. You're going to be the only one on the pool team who doesn't drink.'*

Or·

'Oh all right, if you insist on drinking Coke, why not have a little rum in it, or a little taste of vodka? That won't hurt you.'

You're really going to give yourself a hard time if you're going to change your drinking behaviour, and still go back to old drinking places. You can't expect your drinking partners to understand, because they may not be experiencing what you've been experiencing. As far as they're concerned, everything is OK. If they *have* been behaving the way you have been behaving, they still may not be ready to do what you're doing, so you can't expect them to be of any help other than to help you get back on to the old treadmill again. That's exactly what will happen if you don't give yourself enough time away from that old environment, because initially you won't be strong enough to resist its temptations.

I'm not saying that you'll never be able to go into a pub, club or wherever there's alcohol again – of course you will, but you've got to give yourself every available opportunity to get a good start. One of the best ways to do that is not to surround yourself with temptation. You're only human after all, and if you do put yourself in a situation where you're going to lose face because you're not going to have a drink, you'll probably have just one drink (you think). Then it all starts again, and very quickly – before you know it – you're back where you were.

You may feel that I'm trying to take you away from your friends. What you've got to look at is what sort of friends they are. If they're friends you only see when you're drinking, then they'll be drinking friends. If they are old and trusted friends that you've known for a long time, then I'm sure there'll be other places where you can see them outside of the pub or club. If they're good friends, as you think they are, they may be very supportive of what you're going to do.

Initially I wasn't going to spend so much time talking about not going to pubs and clubs, and what your friends will think, but these were things that worried me when I was giving up drinking, because I thought I'd have nothing left if I didn't go to the pub – I wouldn't have any fun, I wouldn't have any social life, everybody who ever meant anything to me was behind those four walls. I quickly learned that there is a big wide world outside the pub, the club and the off-licence, and that there can be a social life, enjoyment and fun without alcohol being involved.

When you're starting off on these big changes, it's very hard to believe that there's anything other than what you're doing at the moment, so you'll just have to trust me on this one. Don't worry, it will very quickly become apparent that I'm telling the truth.

One of the most important parts of letting go is forgiving yourself and learning to like yourself, learning to accept yourself, finding out who you are rather than who you've been trying to be. You've walked a long road to get here, and along the way you've picked up many negative attitudes towards yourself. You may have done lots of things that you're not proud of or that you feel very ashamed and sad about. You can't carry that bag of old feelings around with you. The more you think about them, the heavier and heavier they'll become. You have to give yourself another chance or else you'll stay stuck in the darkness of your past actions. That's not to say that whatever you did was right, but how long are you supposed to feel bad for it? How long are you supposed to punish yourself for?

You can make amends for a lot of things that've happened in the past, and possibly you'll be able to put things right with the people that you've hurt or upset. The first person you've got to make amends to, however, is yourself, and that's the first part of letting go. Forgive yourself – you've got to give yourself another chance. You deserve another chance, but this time you've got to give it your all. You're going to need all your strength and all your determination to make this time different from all the other times when you've tried to do something about your drinking. Forgiving yourself means that you're going to wipe the slate clean, and give yourself another chance.

Let me give you a word of advice on making amends. When I first quit drinking, I wanted to tell everyone how sorry I was for upsetting them, or for whatever it was I'd done. I found that I got a lot of mixed reactions. I took this as rejection initially, because I didn't understand that there wasn't much trust for me. People had heard it all before – all my promises and commitments never to behave badly again – and of course I'd always gone back to my old ways. So people were very wary of me at first – and rightly so. They'll also be wary of you. So give yourself some time. Get the 'house inside' in order before you start showing people around. Get rid of the garbage and the skeletons that are hidden in the cupboards – have a good emotional clean-out.

You'll probably need some help with this. As I said in Chapter 18, there's plenty of help available – either in self-help groups or in one-to-one counselling, or you can confide in someone who you trust. (If you're a person with faith, this might be a minister or priest.)

Letting go of the old secrets, resentments, fears and hurts that have been torturing you is going to create a lot of room for new things in your life, such as the freedom to choose; the freedom to say 'No'; the right to find yourself, to discover things about yourself, to realize all the potential that you've had for so long that's been unused.

There are many directions you can go in. For once in your life, in the clear light of day, you can actually make some changes – even if that just means walking past the pub to start with (what about that for a change!) instead of that magnet drawing you inside its doors. Imagine what it's like to wake up with a clear head in the morning and with a mouth that doesn't feel as if a camel has fallen asleep in it! Imagine shaving without risking hara-kiri with the razor. Imagine promising your children that you're going to do something with them, and the surprise on their faces when you actually do. See the joy on the faces of people who love you as they watch you let go of that old behaviour and transform into someone you've really always been.

Letting go is hard work. Don't think for a minute that this is going to be easy. It's going to be one of the biggest challenges that's ever been thrown at you, but it's your first step on to new ground that isn't tainted with old memories and old fears. You deserve the chance. Go for it.

22 Taking off the blinkers

The reason why racehorses wear blinkers is to keep their attention focused on only one thing – running the race, going straight ahead and putting all their efforts and energies into winning. If you think about it, you've been doing pretty much the same thing with your drinking. You've been making every effort to keep doing it, and you haven't let anything else distract you from it. Think of the time, energy and commitment you've given to it.

If you're doing something which many people think you shouldn't be doing, a lot of your energy goes into justifying it. Think about how hard you've been working and trying to *win* with your alcohol.

I've yet to meet someone with a drinking problem who has beaten the alcohol, and who can continue to drink without any of the consequences or problems they were experiencing before. It's time to take off the blinkers. It's time to start running another race – a race that you have a chance of winning. The big difference in this race is that people won't be running against you, they'll be running with you. The aim will be to support you. They'll want to help you win the race, and there won't be just one prize, there'll be many – and they'll keep on coming. Things will just keep getting better and better – but first you have to make a decision: you have to make the decision to take off the blinkers.

What can you see at the moment? What prizes are you getting from continuing to drink? How good is your life? Are you really happy with the way things are at present? Is this what you want? Is this what the people who love you want?

As I've said throughout the book, your drinking involves other people: it's not just your problem. That's why there'll be so many people egging you on to do something about it. But it's the same old story – the decision to change has got to come from you. So, are you ready to take off the blinkers? Are you ready to have a look around to see what you've been missing? You've been missing a lot. If there's one message I always hear from people who've quit drinking, it's, 'Why did I take so long to quit? Why didn't I do this earlier? Look what I've been missing – the fun and excitement of life.'

You've also been missing true happiness – not the false version induced by alcohol. Real feelings. Real self-worth. A renewed sense of ambition. Realistic goals rather than unattainable fantasies. Being able to hold your head up – looking people straight in the eye. Looking in the mirror and saying, 'It's all right to be me. Today I'm worth something. I'm not a loser. I'm a winner, and I'm going to stay that way a day at a time with no days off.'

If it's fear that's holding you back from taking off the blinkers, then let's have a look at that fear. What are you frightened of losing? Do you think you're going to lose yourself? Do you think you're not going to be any fun any more? Do you think you'll lose your sense of humour? In fact do you think that alcohol actually gives you a sense of humour? I've yet to see a bottle with the following messages printed on the label:

'WILL HELP WITH HUMOUR'

'WILL MAKE YOU A MORE SOCIABLE, FUN-LOVING PERSON'

'WILL HELP YOUR EYESIGHT AND HELP YOU TO
DRIVE BETTER'

'DRINK THIS AND IT'LL MAKE YOU A MUCH
BETTER PARENT'

'DRINK THE WHOLE LOT AND YOU'LL BE EMPLOYEE OF THE
MONTH . . . HUSBAND OF THE YEAR . . . MOTHER OF THE
YEAR . . . THE MOST RELIABLE FRIEND YOU COULD HAVE
. . . THE BEST PLAYER ON THE TEAM . . .'

It may sound as if I'm trying to be funny, but I'm not. Alcohol doesn't make you any of these things. If anything, it makes you the opposite. So let's get rid of those fears. You're not going to lose yourself, you're going to find yourself. You're not going to lose your sense of humour. You're going to be someone who's worth *being* around – who's worth having as a friend or as an employer or as a member of the team. You're going to be someone who's dependable and trustworthy, and worth having as a husband/wife/father/ mother. Someone who people will be proud of, and happy to say so.

You can make all the excuses you want, but I know for a fact that, whatever it is you think you're good at when you drink, you'll be ten times better without it. 'How can he be so sure?' you may ask. Quite simply because I watch people finding this out every day. Countless people are taking off the blinkers and realizing that there is life without a drink, and that it is possible to succeed with their own strength rather than the false strength that alcohol gives. It's time to break out of the delusion you've been under for so long. It's time to stop just *existing* and start *being*.

How many people do you know who drink like you do? If it's that wonderful, everybody would be at it, but they're not. It's time to change your team. It's time to make a decision.

You may ask what you're going to see when you take off these blinkers. Well, I don't know where to start in answering that question – there are so many things you've been missing out on.

If you have a family, you'll notice how much you've missed while your children have been growing up. You'll notice how many decisions your family have had to make without you, because you've not been available. You'll quickly realize how difficult it's been for them. All of this can be a very positive thing, because it can give you the strength to take responsibility, and to show them what you're willing to do. But it'll take a while, because you're going to have to build up trust again. You can't realistically expect to stop doing the thing you've been doing for a long time, which has been causing problems in your family, and for everything to suddenly be all right. Remember all the times you've said that things would be different, and remember the promises you've made. You've got to give your family a chance to adjust to this new way of life, and for them to get over the hurt that's been caused because of your dependence on alcohol. If you stick to your decision, things will get better and you'll have your family. You'll be a part of what happens in your children's lives. Imagine what it'll be like for them to get their father or mother back.

If you're a son or a daughter, imagine how delighted your parents are going to be at getting their child back. (It doesn't matter how old you are, you'll always be their child in the eyes of your parents!) Think of how proud they're going to be that you've had the courage to do what you're doing.

If you're on your own, then you need to ask yourself why you're on your own. If it's not through choice, then it may be because of your drinking. It may be because you can't find anyone who's willing to put up with your behaviour, or 'it may be because the only relationship you've ever had is with alcohol. I know that feeling.

Another thing you'll see when you take off the blinkers is how much time has been wasted. You'll see how much there is to do. You'll find new interests, or you'll take up some of the old interests that fell by the wayside.

You may be in trouble financially because of your drinking, but the minute you stop you'll instantly be better off and in a much better position to put yourself back on the rails. One reason why you're continuing to drink may be because you really don't want to face up to the financial situation you're in. But you've got to face up to it, because it's not going to get any better if you don't. You'll instantly be better off the minute you quit drinking.

Remember what we've talked about: a concept that has been used repeatedly throughout this book is 'taking responsibility'. When you take off the blinkers, that's exactly what you're doing: you're taking responsibility for the way things are, and you're going to do something about it.

One of the biggest reliefs you're going to feel is the release from fear – the fear you wake up with every day. It's very difficult to explain, and even harder to put it down on paper, but you know what I'm talking about. That fear you feel when you wake up in the middle of the night, and in those sober moments you have. The fear that you can't grasp, but which is there, eating away at you. Maybe it's self-doubt, insecurity, that nagging voice that tells you you're no good, you're not worth anything, you'll never be anything, you'll never achieve anything, you'll never be successful, you'll never be as good or the same as anyone else. Maybe it's that feeling of emptiness when the alcohol wears off. It burns inside you, and no matter how much you drink you can never put that fire out. Even if you drink yourself into oblivion, you still wake up with that same feeling and you have to go through another day with it. The only way you know how to deal with it is to have a drink, but that doesn't take it away. You're stuck with it – that feeling, that fear. I can't tell you what the relief of not having that any more is like. It's beyond words. You've got to experience it for yourself – and you will.

Another thing you'll see is how much better you start to feel physically and just how much more interest you begin to take in yourself and your appearance.

You'll sleep very differently. You'll wake up feeling much more rested, because it will have been a natural sleep rather than the unconscious state that alcohol creates.

Ironically, you'll very quickly realize that giving up is not as bad as you thought it was going to be. I say 'ironically' because one of the overriding reasons why you didn't quit before may have been that you thought that life without alcohol would be terrible and no fun: that it was just going to be all doom and gloom. Maybe you've stopped before. Maybe you were forced to stop. Maybe you stopped under threat from your wife/husband/employer etc. The real difference is that this time *you're* making the decision to quit, which will make it so much easier – the motivation is coming from you rather than from other people. Remember, you can always change your mind – you have the right to do that – but I think you should at least give yourself the chance to find out what your life can be like without alcohol.

Throughout this book you've been doing assignments on how your drinking has affected different areas of your life. What you don't really know yet is what your life will be like without it. I've given you insights and many examples from my own and other people's experiences, but the only way you're really going to experience this is to find out for yourself. This is such a positive way to approach it, because:

a) you're making the decision, and

b) you have the right to change your mind – nobody can take that away from you.

However, you have to be aware that the responsibility is yours and that you have to accept the consequences if you do choose to go back to what you've been doing.

If you're reading this book thinking, 'This is pointless. Nothing's going to change if I stop drinking,' why do you think that? How can you say that when you haven't tried? If you have tried before, you need to ask yourself why you started drinking again. Why didn't you give it more time? What didn't you do? Did you look for help? Did you ask for support? Did you stick it out when things weren't so easy, or did you just fall back into the same old pattern as before? We're talking about you making a major decision – taking off the blinkers and having a look around; having a look at your life;

having a look at your past; having a look at your behaviour, at responsibilities that haven't been taken. More importantly, we're talking about you having a future – a future of happiness, fulfilment and choice. Imagine having the choice to say 'No' to a drink, and actually meaning it and wanting to make that choice.

This may sound very far away or totally unrealistic to you at the moment, but all that's really getting in the way is the need for you to make a decision and put your all into it. Don't listen to that negative voice in your head telling you that you can't do it, or you're not worth it – that's bullshit. You know it and I know it. I haven't met anybody who hasn't been capable of recovery from their dependence upon alcohol. The only thing that got in the way was having to make the decision of actually *wanting* to give up.

So ask yourself: have you had enough of this race? How long have you been in it? What's it's like to keep coming last, to fall at all the jumps? How about taking off the blinkers and joining the rest of us winners? So let's go. You're under starter's orders.

23 Affirmations

I've spent a lot of time talking to you about how you feel. I think it's important to continue along this path and to begin to consider how most people who use alcohol suffer from feelings of inadequacy and inferiority which the outside world may not always recognize.

I've known many people – judges, musicians, parents, artists, businessmen, ministers, doctors, psychiatrists – who on the surface look successful but whose talents and successes mean nothing to them because they can't allow themselves to acknowledge them. Alternatively they'll say, 'Yes, that was good, but I could've done it better,' or 'Yes, I can see I've done a good job, but it doesn't seem to make me very happy.' This low self-worth is like a leech which sucks you dry. It needs to be removed and the wound allowed to heal.

I see getting well as repairing relationships, stopping alcohol from running your life, and becoming physically and mentally stronger. The basis for all of this is, first and foremost, repairing the relationship with yourself. This means continuing to forgive and continuing to accept yourself. I hope that one day you'll even like yourself.

When I was drinking, I hated myself and the way I behaved. I would be obnoxious and rude to people. I was totally self-centred and would never listen to anyone's opinion but my own. Nine times out of ten that opinion was wrong. I was so bad-tempered and angry – I would create situations just to be difficult. Even while I was doing that, somewhere inside of me I knew that it was wrong, but I couldn't do anything about it because the alcohol had such a hold on me. Once I had had a drink, I had no control over what was going to happen.

When I first stopped drinking I had really strong feelings of guilt and remorse for the way I'd behaved, but I had to let the past be just that. I had to live for the day and the next day. I also had to look at what I had, rather than dwelling on my faults. One of the biggest hurdles for me to overcome was to affirm myself.

I have affirmed you many times for sticking with me throughout this book. I will also affirm you for completing the assignments, because I know many of them will have been painful and difficult for you – you've had to look at the reality of your drinking and what the abuse of alcohol has brought into your life.

Do you remember that in Chapter 15 I asked you to take a photograph of yourself? Well, I would like you to take another one at this stage and paste the two down side by side. Then take another one in about three to four weeks' time, and so on. No matter how small, it is really important for you to write down the changes you see.

I still keep the photograph that was taken of me on the day I went into treatment. When I look in the mirror today, I see a totally different person. Before, I was beaten and looked like the walking dead. It was a picture of someone who was broken – my eyes had no sparkle, the veins in my cheeks were red and broken, my face was puffy, my neck was red: I looked exactly how I felt – at the end of the road.

What physical changes do you see? Have a look at your face – is it less puffy, less red? Do you look healthier? Do you look more peaceful and less tense? Has your face filled out because you're eating well now? Have you lost weight if you were overweight? How do your eyes look? Are they clear? Are they sparkling? How is your gaze? Does it look more direct? Are you holding your head more upright because you're feeling better about yourself? Does your smile (if there is one) look more genuine? No matter how *small*, note the changes for the better. It's important to take time to feel better about yourself.

Next I want you to take a long, hard look at yourself. Write down what you like about yourself physically, and what you like about yourself as an individual. Please put some time into this. You need to learn to focus positively on yourself. It might be time also to consider how you've been looking after yourself. Being good to yourself is about taking care of your appearance and your health. You need to take a pride in yourself. When was the last time you went to the doctor, dentist, chiropodist? Do you need a complete overhaul of your appearance? Why not fix up a trip to the hairdresser's? Why not consider your clothes? You can smarten up simply by looking at your standards of hygiene and cleanliness, and see if they need improving.

How physically active are you? Does this need to be improved to get you into better health? I doubt that you've had time to keep yourself fit while you've been abusing yourself with alcohol, so again affirm yourself for taking the time to be good to yourself, and note the changes over the next few weeks. Don't expect too much – it's the little things that count.

If you've been taking yourself for granted, stop it now. Write a list of what you achieve in one day, and keep adding to it. Also affirm yourself for trying, even if you don't succeed 100 per cent.

Where's your sense of humour? Don't think for one moment that this needs to be lost. Isn't this one of the things you're getting sober for? If it's going to be all doom and gloom, what's the point? My sense of humour has never left me, and it's kept me going. Use yours and affirm yourself.

In past chapters I've told you on numerous occasions that having a problem with alcohol doesn't make you a bad person. You need to be aware of where alcohol took you – if you remember that, you won't go back there again.

At this stage you also need to look at the good things you've done in your life. Think of when you've been kind, generous, courteous and caring. That person hasn't gone away – you've just been in the grip of something far stronger than you imagined.

You need to start playing life as a winner – go after the new goals in your life with persistence and a resolve to succeed. It may feel like hard work – it is hard work – but be honest with yourself: how easy was the drinking and all that went with it – the lies, the deceit, the covering-up, the excuses, the minimizing, the manipulation, the blaming, the rationalizations? How much energy did all that take? All you need to do is use that energy to win. With each new goal you've chosen, remember always to be reasonable and realistic – don't set your goals too high, but don't fear success. Yes, you heard me right. We who've turned to alcohol often have a fear of being well, and an even greater fear of success. I want you to think really hard about this. Watch out for the old habits. Remember how good you are at sabotaging yourself and getting in the way of your doing well. Be careful of this old behaviour.

Positive changes mean living up to greater expectations, but think of the rewards – you can become a winner, so don't get caught up in that old game of self-defeat. When you don't win, please don't see your set-backs in terms of failure. Examining where you went wrong can be a real source of learning and of growth. This can be true even if you pick up a drink after a period of sobriety. Look at what happened and what you weren't doing. Look after yourself rather than beating yourself up. It's hard to be positive, and even harder to affirm yourself if you're holding on to the past. It's like dragging a lot of full black bin-bags around with you. It's like having blinkers on your eyes and cotton wool in your ears, stopping you seeing the present and hearing affirmations. How can you stand up straight when you're carrying so much old luggage full of resentments around with you?

If you have resentments, draw up a list of what's bugging you. Have a good look at it, and ask whether you'd be happier to put these things in the past or to hang on to them. Imagine being free of them. Imagine having that weight taken off you. It will feel like such an enormous relief after having dragged it around for so long. Your self-esteem will be immediately enhanced, because you'll be kicking the habit of seeing yourself as that tragic figure who has suffered for so long and been so badly wronged.

Resentments are a trap that will lead you back to the bottle: they are an instant recipe for relapse. You have to be very careful about getting resentful. Once you get caught up in this old behaviour, it's like trying to swim against a current that's going the other way. Very quickly you get tired, and before you know it you're being swept back to where you started. If you're looking after yourself and not trying to do too much too soon, you'll be OK. You'll have ups and downs – that's life – but look at the way your life is going to change.

Getting into the habit of affirming yourself on a daily basis is going to be a very important part of your recovery, so start as you mean to go on. Remember what I said earlier about how low self-worth is like a leech which needs to be removed and the wound allowed to heal. Don't forget how long you've been wounded. It's going to need a lot of attention on a *daily basis* – even if it's only looking in the mirror in the morning and saying, 'I'm all I've got, and that's OK.' Don't forget where you've come from and you won't quickly go back there again.

Start affirming yourself today – you're worth getting better for. Well done.

24 Tomorrow I'll be different

How many times have you said to someone, 'Tomorrow I'll be different. This'll never happen again. I really mean it this time – I'm going to stop drinking, and not another drop is going to touch my lips. Just you wait and see'? So they waited, and waited, and what did they see? The same old story. The same old pattern. The same old behaviour all over again.

I do believe that you really meant it when you said you'd never do it again, that it was all over and you were sorry for what you'd done. Nevertheless, there may also have been a part of you that was saying that to keep people off your back, because you didn't remember exactly what had happened, or what you'd done, because you were in a blackout. I don't mean that you were lying unconscious or that you'd fainted: I mean that you were in an alcohol-induced blackout – you couldn't remember what had taken place.

How many times have you woken up after a night's drinking and thought to yourself, 'How did I get home last night? Did I drive? Did somebody drive me? Where did I leave the car? How did I get into bed? I can't remember taking off my clothes?' Maybe you've woken up somewhere else but you can't remember how you got there.

Another scenario could be that you wake up in the morning and your wife/husband/boyfriend/girlfriend isn't talking to you. You say to them, 'What's wrong? What've I done? Why aren't you talking to me?' They look at you disbelievingly and say, 'Why aren't I talking to you? After what you did and what happened?' You stand there with a blank look on your face and say, 'What do you mean "what I did"?' They in turn say, 'Oh come on! Don't give me that. You know exactly what you did! How could you behave like that? How could you say those things?' But you're still thinking, 'What did I do?'

Maybe you've been out with friends for the evening. You see them the following day and they're being offhand with you. You ask them why, and again they look at you disbelievingly and say, 'Why? I'll tell you why!', and they reel off the events of the night before. You listen to this thinking, 'Oh no! Did I say that? Did I do those things? Did I behave like that?', and somewhere inside there's a voice saying, 'Yes, you did.' You feel awful and remorseful, but that doesn't change the situation, does it? It still happened. You behaved like that yet again.

At the other end of the scale, you may have woken up in a police station because you'd been drunk and disorderly or drunk in charge of your car. Maybe you got into a fight with someone, or maybe you were found asleep somewhere. Whatever the situation, when you open your eyes you have difficulty piecing together last night's events.

In the past you may have thought this was funny. Or some

of your drinking friends may have said to you, 'Guess what you did last night! That was really funny!' But when you hear it, it doesn't sound funny at all – it sounds embarrassing, but there's nothing you can do: it's happened. It isn't funny at all, is it?

What's happening is that when you have a certain amount to drink you lose control over how you're going to behave, and that means that anything can happen. This is serious, because it also means that you don't have a choice: the moment you have that first drink, you don't have any control over what's going to happen. In fact this is more than serious – it's terrifying, because not only does it mean that you don't know what's going to happen, but other people around you don't know either. Imagine what that feels like.

So there you are, on one of those mornings, and you're saying, 'I promise it won't happen again. I'll never have another drink as long as I live. You know I didn't mean to say those things. You know how much I care about you. I love you.' Empty bottles and broken promises raining down on the ears of people who've heard them all before, but you stand there and make the same promises over and over again. You wonder why they don't believe you! It's all so sad, because the alcohol is taking your dignity, your self-respect, your morale and your values and juggling with them. It's getting to the stage where you don't know what's going to be dropped next, or what you're going to be left with.

Is it worth it? Of course it's not worth it, but you can't even think of it in those terms any more, can you? It's not social drinking any more, or the occasional drink: we're talking about dependence. We're talking about a situation where you can't live with alcohol but you just can't seem to live without it. No matter what it does to you, you want to keep picking it up. You've got to stop deluding yourself into thinking that you can still control this and that you're still in charge. In fact that should be simple for you – all you have to do is look back over the assignments I've given you in this book and you'll have a very clear picture of what's been happening. Maybe you don't want to look. Maybe you want to give drinking another go. Maybe you're not ready. Maybe you have to suffer some more consequences. What worries me is that dying may be one of them. You can't tell me that won't happen, because you don't know. You're not special and different in this respect – you're one of countless people who have this problem, and unless you do something about it it's going to get worse.

If you've made the decision that you want to do something about your drinking problem, then well done – you've made a decision that's going to save your life. If you're willing to work hard enough to make the changes you need to, you'll get the benefits in all aspects of your life. Instead of being broken, promises can actually come true. You really can recover from your dependence on alcohol and live a much happier life without it.

Initially this is not going to be easy, and you're going to need all the help, support and guidance you can get. One of the first steps I can advise you to take is to go to see your doctor. Tell him or her what you're deciding to do and why. You might have been to see your doctor before and talked about your drinking, and you may have played down the amount you've been drinking. No matter: it's time to go again and make it clear what you're going to do. The level of your alcohol abuse may mean that you need some medical attention, so it's important that you have a check-up. You may also experience withdrawals because of the amount of alcohol you've been drinking, and there again your doctor will be able to help you. Don't take any chances or cut corners with your health. Remember, you're turning over a new leaf. You're taking responsibility for yourself, and your health comes first.

Don't expect your family and friends to jump up and down when you tell them you're going to quit drinking – remember, they've heard it all before. Don't feel disappointed with their reaction, and don't get angry. To help you with this, look back over the assignments you've completed in this book and look at the way you've been behaving. That'll help you understand why you're getting this reaction. It's going to take time, but their trust will come as you get stronger and as the days go by and they see that you really are making changes. Don't forget that you're not the only one who's recovering from your drinking problem – people close to you have to recover too. It's going to take time to repair the damage that's been done, but you'll get stronger each day without a drink and you'll feel better about yourself. Slowly you'll start to believe in yourself.

After having not believed in yourself for such a long time, you won't want to let go of this feeling. It's priceless to be able to feel good about yourself and to be able to hold your head up and say, 'I'm doing something about me. I'm making some changes.' It feels good, and it drives you on. You'll become protective about your new, sober way of life.

Don't forget that little man on your shoulder, because he's not going to go away. He's never going to give up. He'll seize any opportunity to tell you that you can have a drink. The analogy I use of 'the little man' is really your addiction talking to you, because your addiction isn't going to go away.

One of the biggest mistakes that people with a drinking problem make is to think that because they've stopped drinking for a period of time, because their health and family life have improved, because they're working better and they've re-established a relationship with their friends, they can have a couple of drinks. For someone who is addicted to alcohol, there's no such thing as 'a couple of drinks'. There never was a couple of drinks, so why should it be any different now? If you pick up a drink again, you're picking up the nightmare – only there's a twist in it: you don't pick up where you left off. You'll be plunged very quickly into a dark hole, because that's the only direction in which your addiction will lead you. I don't say this from personal experience, because to this day I've not picked up a drink after quitting, but I've worked with people who have relapsed with alcohol. They've told me their experiences and how almost immediately they were in trouble with their drinking again – but it wasn't the same as before for them; it was worse. I can't warn you against this strongly enough.

It's very easy to forget where you've come from, but it's easier still to go back there if you do. As I write this book I'm going into my tenth year without a drink, but I've not forgotten the nightmare. I've not forgotten how I felt when I was going through the withdrawals from my drinking. I'll never forget those feelings of worthlessness, remorse and shame, and that despair each morning when I opened my eyes not knowing what was going to happen to me. I'll never forget wondering if my hand would ever stop shaking when I lifted it. I'll never forget the constant feeling of insecurity because I couldn't survive without a drink and yet I couldn't survive with one. I hope and pray that I'll keep those memories with me until the day I die, because they'll help me and keep me from picking up a drink again. I can honestly say that most days I don't feel like a drink. As time goes on it gets easier and easier and easier, but, as I've said, don't forget where you've come from and you won't easily go back there again.

Please have another look at Chapter 18. Through that you'll be able to find the support that you need to help you through your difficult times of not drinking. Help is not far away. All you have to do is pick up the phone before you pick up a drink.

It may not seem like it, but at this moment you're making a decision towards freedom. By not picking up another drink, you're going to break free of the obsession and compulsion that's been driving you to destroy yourself. Today's decision is tomorrow's freedom – freedom from all that darkness you've been in; freedom to see some light, to have some future, to have success. No matter what you do, no matter who you are, no matter what your background, you deserve the chance to live and to make the best possible life for yourself and those around you. You can do this. One day at a time, with no days off, you can succeed without having to drink. You'll experience happiness and contentment as time goes on.

You'll also have something in your life which you've never had before, which is – quite simply – choice:

- The choice not to drink.
- The choice to better yourself.
- The choice to care for yourself and the people around you.
- The choice to tell others how you've been able to help yourself, so that maybe they'll be able to help themselves.
- The choice, most of all, to make some changes, so that tomorrow you really will be different.

Key to questionnaire on pages 23–5

Six or more 'Yes' answers indicate some level of dependency on alcohol.